HOLY GHOST & SPIRITUAL GIFTS

CONNIE JACKSON

WESTBOW
PRESS®
A DIVISION OF THOMAS NELSON
& ZONDERVAN

This book is a work of non-fiction. Unless otherwise noted, the author
and the publisher make no explicit guarantees as to the accuracy of
the information contained in this book and in some cases, names of
people and places have been altered to protect their privacy.

WestBow Press books may be ordered through booksellers or by contacting:

WestBow Press
A Division of Thomas Nelson & Zondervan
1663 Liberty Drive
Bloomington, IN 47403
www.westbowpress.com
844-714-3454

Scripture taken from the King James Version of the Bible.

ISBN: 978-1-6642-6008-5 (sc)
ISBN: 978-1-6642-6007-8 (e)

Print information available on the last page.

WestBow Press rev. date: 03/04/2022

A STUDY GUIDE FOR THE BAPTISM OF THE HOLY SPIRIT AND THE NINE GIFTS OF THE HOLY SPIRIT

Notes for this study compiled by:
Pastor Connie Jackson
2019

CONTENTS

This book was written with the intention of giving the members of my church, Victory Tabernacle, a better understanding, and knowledge of the baptism of the Holy Spirit and the working of the nine gifts of the Holy Spirit. I prayerfully compiled the notes for a teaching series on this subject. My studies came from God's word and from teaching that I listened to from Pastor Perry Stone.

Our scripture text for this series of study is found in First Corinthians 12:1-11. The list for the nine gifts are given in verses eight through ten. I did not teach this series in the order given in the text, but I taught according to the division of the gifts. You will find the list of the divisions I used with a short definition for each gift on the following page.

After receiving many requests for copies of my notes, I have put them together into this book, in hopes that they will be a blessing and an encouragement to those who read it. It is my earnest desire to see a great outpouring of God's spirit in our churches today. While I was praying for this, I felt my spirit being nudged with the thought, people will not seek for something they don't understand.

It is my hope that the teaching in this book will help to bring a better understanding, prompting a greater desire for a mighty move of God in our local churches and throughout the land. We serve a mighty God, and he has not changed.

The Mind Gifts	The Power Gifts	The Vocal Gifts
Word of Wisdom	Works of Miracles	Diverse Tongues
Word of Knowledge	Gifts of Healing	Prophecy
Discerning of Spirits	Faith	Interpretation of Tongues

The Holy Spirit is the giver of the following gifts and distributes them as He pleases.

1. Word of Wisdom: A God-inspired instruction giving supernatural wisdom to solve problems.
2. Word of Knowledge: the supernatural ability to receive, comprehend, and distribute spiritual information.
3. Discerning of Spirits: to discern and distinguish the human spirit, the Spirit of God, or spirits from Satan.
4. Working of Miracles: the supernatural ability to pray and experience miraculous answers in prayer.
5. Gifts of Healing: the supernatural ability to minister healing to others using all New Testament methods.
6. Faith: the supernatural ability to believe for the impossible without doubting or wavering.
7. Divers Tongues (or divers): the supernatural ability to speak in other tongues, or languages, through the Holy Spirit's utterance.
8. Prophecy: the supernatural ability to speak forth a right-now word for edification, exhortation, and comfort.
9. Interpretation of Tongues: the supernatural ability to interpret into the native tongue the words of diverse tongues.

INTRODUCTION

I would like for us to begin this study with the understanding that God is a God of order. If we go all the way back to the beginning and read the first chapter of Genesis, we find that from the first day God had an order and a plan for all of creation. He didn't rush through it, but took his time, much like an artist painting a masterpiece. He brought order out of chaos. He brought light into the darkness and separated time and space. He spoke into each day exactly what was needed for that day and in the order that it was needed. Think about it this way, the water didn't need the fish to exist, but the fish needs the water. Creation of each day was planned and put into place for what was coming in the next day. Ending with the creation of man and woman on the sixth day and resting on the seventh.

Now let's move on up to the sixth chapter of Genesis where we find that sin has taken over on the earth. Things had gotten so bad after the fall of man in the garden that God's heart was grieved, and he decides to destroy man and beast. But one man was still holding on to God. The bible says in Genesis 6:8 that Noah found grace in the eyes of the Lord. So, God speaks to Noah. Notice that God is very precise in his directions to Noah. He doesn't want Noah to just gather some wood and build a big boat without instruction. But in Genesis 6:14-16 God gives very detailed instruction on how to accomplish this command and why. Noah was given exact measurements on how long, how wide, and how tall this structure was to be. He was told what kind of wood to use and how to pitch it with tar to make it watertight. God instructed him on how many cubicles he would need to make for the animals and the size for each one. He told him how much provision he would need for the amount of time that he would be on the ark. Once the animals, Noah, and his family were safely inside, God shut the door and the rain came.

We could continue to look all throughout the bible and find examples of God's order. Not only did he give Noah the blueprint for the ark, but he also gave Moses direct and precise directions for setting up the tabernacle in the wilderness. He gave him the measurements, as well as the kind and color of the materials to be used. If you look at Exodus chapter ten, you will see that God even told him what day it was to be done on and where to place the furniture. Exodus 10:2-5; On the first day of the first month shalt thou set up the tabernacle of the tent of the congregation. And thou shalt put therein the ark of the testimony and cover the ark with the veil. And thou shalt bring in the table and set in order the things that are to be set in order upon it; and thou shalt bring in the candlestick and light the lamps thereof. And thou shalt set the altar of gold for the incense before the ark of the testimony and put the hanging of the door to the tabernacle. Very precise instruction and order.

Every time that God's people were faced with opposition or war, he would tell them exactly how to deal with it. If they were marching, he would give them the order for which to line up. When they went into Jericho, he told Joshua what to do to bring the walls down. Nothing is ever haphazard or chaotic with God. As a matter of fact, he states that he is not the author of confusion and will not be a part of it.

So, with all of this in mind, doesn't it stand to reason that when he set up his church, he had a plan and an order for it? He set up ministries, helps and government with the church to see that it was ran in order according to his plan and his purpose. We know that Christ is the head of the church and that if you have an assembly that he is not the head of you are already out of order. Under Christ there are pastors. A pastor should be called and placed in that position by the call of God. When he or she is placed there by God, then he will lead them and give them the direction for the church.

I am not going to get too deep into that right now, because our goal is to get to the understanding of the Holy Spirit along with the nine gifts of the spirit and how they operate in the church. I just wanted to give an understanding that God has an order in place for anything that has his name on it. He gave the Holy Spirit and the nine gifts to the church to empower us for the battles that we must fight in life. However as with everything that God sets, there is an order to receiving and walking in these gifts.

The fundamental foundation for the church has not changed. Jesus said upon this rock I will build my church and the gates of hell shall not prevail against it. Jesus Christ is the rock. He is the foundation, the chief cornerstone. If you don't build on him, you are building in vain.

BAPTISM OF THE HOLY SPIRIT

As with all things that are ordained and given from God there is an order to receiving the baptism of the Holy Spirit and the gifts of the Spirit. The first order of progression toward this baptism is salvation. There are those today who want to skip over salvation and jump right into doing a work for God. They think that if they live good enough, work hard enough, or give enough money, that those things will save them. Jesus teaches us that there is only one way to get to the Father and that is by and through him. He is the door. He is the truth. And he is the way. If we were capable of saving ourselves through our works, he would not have had to go to the cross. Jesus not only paid the price for our salvation, but he made it so simple that anyone can receive it. In Romans 10:9 it says, that if thou shalt confess with thy mouth the Lord Jesus, and shalt believe in thine heart that God hath raised him from the dead, thou shalt be saved. It's as easy as knowing your ABC's. **A**dmit you are a sinner, **B**elieve that Jesus died for your sins, and **C**onfess that he is Lord. There are some who teach today that when you get saved you are automatically baptized in the Holy Spirit. While that can and sometimes does happen, it is not always the case. When you surrender your heart to God, his spirit does come in and you are sealed by his spirit, however it is not the same as when you receive the baptism of the Holy Spirit. We will talk more about this later in the book.

The second thing that you need is sanctification. I realize that this is not a popular subject and that it is not often taught on, but it is still necessary for progression in the things of God. Sanctification is spoken of in both the Old and the New Testaments. We can look at Joshua in the Old Testament as he is preparing to lead the people over Jordan into the promised land. In the book of Joshua 3:5, he says; sanctify yourselves; for tomorrow the Lord will do wonders among you. Then if you look in the New Testament at first Thessalonians 5:23, it says; and the very God of peace sanctify you Holy and I pray God your whole spirit, soul and body be preserved blameless unto the coming of the Lord Jesus Christ. To sanctify means to set apart. To be set apart for a Holy purpose or a Holy use. After you have given your heart to the Lord and received salvation, there is a cleansing process that begins. I say begins because sanctification is an ongoing process.

Sanctification is not an instantaneous once in a lifetime process. There is a cleansing that begins at the time of salvation, and it continues throughout your walk with God. Think about this, when a new baby is born, one of the first things done is cleaning it up. It gets wiped off initially and then after it is checked out it is given it's first of many baths. When someone surrenders their heart to God and asks Jesus into their heart, they become a spiritual newborn. Since the birth is spiritual so is the cleansing. Some things are taken away instantly as the transformation takes place while others have to be dealt with through time and conviction. Have you seen people who say they are saved and live a Christian life but still have habits in their life? They knelt at an altar and surrendered their heart and life to God, but they are still struggling with these strong holds in their life. It takes the anointing of God to break a bondage and destroy the yoke that people have allowed to have control in their lives. I heard T.D. Jakes preach it like this once; When Jesus called Lazarus from the tomb, he gave him life, but he still had the grave clothes on. Jesus then said to those standing around, "loose him and set him free." So, Jesus saves them and gives them new life, but then he tells the church to do its part in getting them loosed and set free. We do that through teaching them, (by example, living it before them), praying for them and teaching them through the word of God what is expected of them. It is not our job to condemn but to allow the Holy Spirit to convict. Having said that, some people believe that once you are set free from a habit or from whatever had you bound, that you are now baptized in the Holy Spirit. But no, that is when you have begun to become sanctified. As I said before sanctification is an ongoing process. Paul said, "I die daily." How often do you take a bath in the natural? It's the same in the spiritual. Things slip in, things happen. We need to allow the Holy Spirit to search our hearts and cleanse us daily.

I got saved in a little Pentecostal church when I was around ten years of age and grew up under the ministry of Reverend Georgia B. Hughes, who was the Pastor at that time, and this is how we were taught. Holy Ghost filled people would testify, "I thank God that I am saved, sanctified, and filled with the Holy Ghost." We knew that you had to go through each level in order to reach the goal of the baptism of the Holy Ghost. And it was impressed upon us not to get satisfied but to continually strive to go farther in our relationship with God. Now day's people seem to be content with salvation and rarely do you see people striving for sanctification and the baptism of the Holy Spirit. That is why we see gossip, back biting, and division in the church. These things require sanctification to get free from. I think this is mostly attributed to a lack of knowledge. Hosea chapter 4 and the beginning of verse six says; My people are destroyed for lack of knowledge: because thou have rejected knowledge, I will reject thee. We must know the steps to God and follow them.

The third step brings us to the baptism of the Holy Spirit or Holy Ghost, whichever way you prefer to say it. Once you have been saved and sanctified, then you are a candidate for the baptism of the Holy Spirit. A question that is often asked is "is there a difference between Holy Ghost and Holy Spirit? Let's talk about ghost verses spirit for a moment. Ghost is the word that the Old King James uses, and Spirit is the word used in newer translations. The older generation like to use the term Holy Ghost because that is what they grew up with. The younger generation say, ghost? That sounds like dead people and spirits that type of ghost, so they prefer Holy Spirit. In the Greek there is no difference. You can say Holy Ghost or Holy Spirit. It is a preference thing for a believer, whichever you are comfortable with or have been taught. Remember that there are unbelievers who have not been taught in the word of God or maybe they haven't been in a church where the Spirit of God moves, and they are confused by it. If you find yourself discussing the Holy Spirit for some reason with someone unfamiliar with him, you might want to clarify the difference between the Holy Spirit and Casper. I know that might sound humorous but in reality, there are some folks who truly don't know or understand what you are talking about.

Another question that people sometimes ask is, "Is there a difference in the baptism and the infilling of the Holy Ghost?" Scripture speaks of both. First let's look at how the Spirit of God worked in the Old Testament. The bible tells us in the Old Testament that the Holy Spirit would come upon an individual, enabling them to perform certain supernatural feats. For example, in Judges 16:3; and 15:16, we see examples of Samson and when the spirit of God came upon him he carried an iron gate up a hill side on his shoulders. Another time when the spirit of God came upon him, he took a jawbone of a donkey and killed a thousand Philistines. In the New Testament the Spirit of God would baptize the believer and not lift from them but abide in them as long as they remain in covenant with God. Now let me give you scripture for being baptized and filled. Matthew 3:11 says; He (Jesus) shall baptize you with the Holy Ghost and with fire. Acts 1:5; Jesus said you shall be (in the future tense) baptized in the Holy Ghost. Now let's look at the word filled in the New Testament. Acts 2:4; On the day of Pentecost one hundred and twenty gathered and they were all filled with the Holy Ghost and began to speak with other tongues as the spirit gave utterance. Acts 4:8; Peter filled with the Holy Ghost said unto them. Acts 9:17: Then Saul who was later called Paul, filled with the Holy Ghost set his eyes upon him. Acts 13:52; and the disciples were filled with the Holy Spirit and with joy.

Now listen to this very carefully. The word baptism, or when we speak of Holy Spirit baptism, we are talking about the first initial act and infilling is the result. Baptism is the initial act, the moment you're baptized, and you speak in the prayer language (another tongue) you are baptized at that moment, but now you are also filled which is a result of baptism. Millions of people have received baptism in the Holy Spirit. Acts 2:1-4; 10:45-46; 19:1-7 are bible examples of some who were filled with the Holy Spirit as the act of baptism.

Let's look at it like this. If you take a glass and fill it with water and compare it to an individual who has accepted Christ as their Savior. You already have the Holy Spirit because the bible says you are born of the spirit. If you are born again, you have Christ in you. Now if we take that glass that is filled with water and stick it in a tub of water, you submerge it, it is now baptized. To cover completely with water. So, baptism of the Holy Spirit is the power of God coming into your spirit, filling you up completely with God's power and anointing and now there is infilling or filled in Him and that is the result of baptism. That is the moment that we can say we have been baptized and are filled with the Holy Spirit. Hopefully that will help you to understand some of the controversy between those two phrases of being baptized and being filled. Baptism is when you feel the saturation of God's Spirit totally engulfing you and it leaves you saturated or filled with His Spirit and power. We need to understand this because we are going to be dealing with the operation of the gifts and why we believe that you must be filled with the Holy Spirit first for the gifts to fully operate in your life.

Another question that is often asked is, "When do I get filled?" Some believe it's at the moment of conversion. They think that when you are converted (saved) you are automatically baptized and filled with the Holy Spirit. John 16:8 says, when he (the Holy Spirit) is come, he will reprove the world of sin and of righteousness and of judgment. Therefore, some people will think, ok now that I have been convicted of sin and repented or converted to Christ, I am now baptized and filled with the Holy Spirit. While it is true that you are born of the Spirit because Jesus tells us in the third chapter of John, that we must be born again of the water and the spirit, it is a little different than being baptized in the spirit. One has to do with redemption and the other has to do with empowering. So, when you are converted and saved, that's one level of being born in the spirit but the empowerment is another level. Luke said it this way; you shall be endued (clothed) with power from on high. So, you have two very distinct things going on. Being born of the spirit (salvation) and the empowering of the spirit (Holy Ghost). Another reference to conversion is found in John 6:44; no man can come unto me except the father who has sent me draw him, and I will raise him up at the last day.

There are some that believe you are filled if you have the Joy of the Lord. Acts 8:15 says; they laid their hands on them and they received the Holy Ghost with great joy in the city. This is when they went down to the city of Samaria and preached Jesus to them, and they were baptized in the Holy Spirit. Notice they said great joy in the city. The bible tells us that the kingdom of God is not meat and drink but righteousness, peace, and joy in the Holy Ghost. Joy is a fruit of the Spirit. Notice it is not listed as one of the nine gifts but peace and joy, in the book of Galatians, are listed in the nine fruits of the Spirit. Joy is a fruit that should come out of you because of your relationship with the Lord Jesus Christ. So yes, the Holy Spirit brings joy and trust me, when you're baptized in the Holy Spirit, there is a whole other level of joy that comes. But while joy will accompany the Holy Spirit, it does not mean that you have been baptized in the Holy Spirit. Remember that there is a difference between being born of the spirit and being baptized in the spirit.

Some believe that you are baptized in the Holy Ghost when you are sanctified. We have already covered that one under sanctification. I would, however, like to say here that there are some people that receive all three at the same time. They get saved, sanctification begins to take place and they are filled with the Holy Ghost. It can and occasionally does happen, but it is rare. Most of the time the baptism of the Holy Ghost is received at different stages depending on the person and their understanding and readiness to receive.

Another question asked is, "how do I know when I am filled?" If we go to the New Testament, there are specific references that tell you how to recognize that you have been and are filled. On the day of Pentecost, in Acts 2:1-4, they are all filled with the Holy Spirit and begin to speak with other tongues as the spirit gave utterance. One of the words used for what we call the prayer language or tongues is *Glossolalia*, meaning to speak in another tongue. In the book of Acts 10:45-46, we read about a gathering at the house of a man named Cornelius. Peter went there and preached, and they were all baptized in the Holy Ghost and began to speak with tongues. This was the same manifestation that the apostles had in Acts chapter 2. In Acts 19:1-12, the disciples of John the Baptist had not even heard that there was a Holy Ghost. Now think about this for a moment. Jesus had preached for three and a half years, he had already been crucified, risen from the dead and ascended to heaven. The day of Pentecost with the Holy Spirit outpouring had occurred but, here in Ephesus, which is in Asia Minor, they had not heard about it. Paul taught them, then he laid hands on them, and they received the baptism of the Holy Ghost, and they spoke with tongues and prophesied.

So, this is three different locations where this is happening. In Acts two it happens in Jerusalem. In Acts ten we see an outpouring in Caesarea, which is on the coast of Israel, in the house of Cornelius. And then in Acts nineteen it reaches Ephesus which is in Asia Minor. What's interesting in all these occurrences is that they had no idea of what was coming. The apostles knew, based on what Jesus said and was later recorded in Mark 3:16, they would speak with new tongues. So, they knew there was something connected to the tongues although they were not aware when or how it was going to happen. Notice in Acts ten that Peter never tells them, now you're about to get saved and speak in tongues. He says nothing about speaking in tongues and yet look what happens to them. They all begin speaking in tongues. In Acts chapter nineteen Paul starts preaching to the disciples of John the Baptist and reminds them about John's prediction that someone would come after him, speaking about Jesus, that would baptize them with Holy Ghost and fire. Once again, Paul never tells them that they are going to speak in tongues and yet as before and in every single instance, what happened? They spoke with tongues. Showing that it had to come directly from the Holy Spirit and not a man motivating them or planting the thought in their mind.

Two more examples are found in chapter eight of the book of Acts. Peter and John were sent to Samaria to pray for some new converts that had not yet received the baptism of the Holy Ghost. When Peter and John laid hands on them, they received the Spirit and a man known as Simon the sorcerer, when he saw it, tried to buy the gift of laying on of hands. Now it doesn't tell you that they spoke in tongues, but something happened because if all he had done was lay his hand on them and all they did was say praise God, hallelujah, then why would Simon want the gift? Simon saw something happen that was so supernatural, that he wanted the gift himself and it stands to reason from all the other examples given that they began to speak in tongues. The last example on this point is Paul. When he first enters the pages of scripture he is known as Saul. We have read and heard it preached many times how that he was struck blind while going to Damascus to persecute the church. After he was blinded, Jesus spoke to him, and told him where to go and wait for a man by the name of Ananias. When Ananias came and laid hands on him and said, "be filled with the Holy Ghost" it doesn't say he spoke in tongues but later in First Corinthians he said, "I thank my God, I speak in tongues more than you all." So, the point is, if we take Acts 2, 10, and 19, which have direct references to the baptism, and if we take Acts chapter 9 about Paul, which gives the implication. According to these references you know when you are baptized in the Holy Spirit, because you do what? You speak with a new tongue. Or you speak in tongues.

Once you have followed these steps and have been filled with the Holy Ghost or Holy Spirit, whichever you prefer to call him. And I would like to clarify that the Holy Ghost is a him. He is the third part of the God head. He is not an it or an apparition, but he is God in Spirit. He's God in the Father, he's God in the Son, he's God in the Holy Ghost and all these three are one. The thought occurred to me as I was writing these notes – saved by the Father – filled and sealed by the son – baptized by the Holy Ghost. Then you are a candidate for the gifts of the spirit that come after the baptism.

WHO IS THE HOLY GHOST AND WHAT IS THE PURPOSE OF THE GIFTS OF THE SPIRIT?

WHO IS THE HOLY GHOST? AS I SAID PREVIOUSLY, HE IS NOT AN IT OR a thing. He is the third part of the God head. The trinity is three separate beings, but they are a package. They are all three in one. I was thinking on how to best explain this. My first thought was to use the analogy of electricity. God wires you just like you wire your house for electricity. There is wiring going all through your house to bring power into it. But until you are connected to the power source, the power is not activated. Jesus is the connection that brings life into the wiring. He said I came to give you life. If you touch a wire that has a connection to the power source, even though you don't see the power, you will definitely feel the power. Now if you want to see the power, you have to turn on the switch and if everything is in place, it will bring forth a visual light or sound etc. The Holy Ghost is your spiritual power switch.

However, while I was thinking about this, I began to get another visual. Do you remember the old coal oil lamps? You have a lamp, which represents the believer. You feel it with oil, which represents God. Then you place a wick, which represents the Lord Jesus Christ. When you receive the baptism of the Holy Ghost, he is a fire that lights the wick, that is saturated in the oil, which fills the lamp. All three work together inside of the believer to bring forth a light into the world that Jesus says in Matthew 5:14-15, we are to be.

Why do we need the Holy Ghost today? In Acts 1:8, Jesus says, "you will receive power after that the Holy Ghost has come upon you: and ye shall be witnesses unto me both in Jerusalem, and in all Judea, and in Samaria, and unto the uttermost part of the earth.

What happened when the disciples were filled with the Holy Ghost on the day of Pentecost? These men who loved Jesus with all of their hearts, but still fled when trouble came. These men that scattered when the law showed up. Peter who denied knowing who Jesus was. After the crucifixion, all of these men, hid behind locked doors because they feared the Jews. But once they received the power of the Holy Ghost, they walked boldly out of the upper room and began to teach and witness to thousands of people. Peter who had denied Christ, became the spokesman, and said let me tell you about my Jesus. These are not drunk as you suppose (how did he know that's what they were saying? He had been in the upper room with the others. The Holy Ghost reveals the hidden things), but this is that which the prophet Joel spoke about. They lost their fear, and they gained a power and authority that they no longer feared the Jews or the law, but they began to speak boldly. God threw the switch and power came on and the world became illuminated with His light.

Holy Ghost power knows no fear of the world because God the Father and God the Son have already conquered the world, and now he is releasing his power into the world through his church, his bride, his children. He is fully connected with those who believe and follow him. When the enemy attacks, the Holy Ghost responds. I saw a perfect demonstration right here in our church during a Sunday morning service. There was a sister sitting in the church, and as I preached, I could feel a spirit of anger and hatred coming from her. I knew that the enemy was attacking her. About the time that I felt to lay hands on her and pray, there was a disturbance that arose from behind her, and the spirit leading me to pray for her lifted. She left angry and I continued to pray for the next two days for her deliverance. The afternoon of the second day, she called me and said, "Pastor, I don't know what happened, but I came under a heavy attack on Sunday morning. I felt such a hatred and anger come over me. I have never felt anything like that before, and I can't explain it, but I went home and began to seek God and I now feel free from it. I apologize for my actions." The enemy comes to steal, to kill, and to destroy and he comes into the house of God with his spirits, and if possible, causes confusion to hinder the move of God. But Jesus said, "I come that you might have life, and have it abundantly."

The Holy Ghost is a fire. Matthew 3:11 and Luke 3:16 both state that John when he was baptizing people said, "I baptize with water of repentance but he that cometh after me is mightier than I, whose shoes I am not worthy to bear, he shall baptize you with Holy Ghost, and with fire." When the Holy Ghost comes in to live, he ignites a fire inside of you. It makes me think of Jeremiah when he said, "I might want to give up, but just as I think I might, there is fire that is shut up in my bones." As long as you keep feeding the fire, he will keep you stirred up for Jesus. You can't get cold if you are keeping your fire stirred and fed. You won't run out, wear out, or burn out if you are walking in close relationship with the Father, Son, and Holy Ghost. It's when you begin to slack on God that coldness creeps in, dissatisfaction appears, anger and jealousy rear up their ugly heads. If you don't squash them, they will continue to grow into monsters that will overshadow you and then overpower you.

The Holy Ghost is a teacher. John 14:26 says; But the comforter, which is the Holy Ghost, whom the father will send in my name, he shall teach you all things, and bring all things to your remembrance, whatsoever I have said unto you. If you read the scriptures and put them inside your heart and mind, not only will he help you to understand what they are saying to you, but he will also pull them up in your mind when they are needed. Matthew 10:19 and 20 says; But when they deliver you up, take no thought how or what ye shall speak: for it shall be given you in that same hour what ye shall speak. For it is not ye that speak, but the Spirit of your Father which speaketh in you.

The Holy Ghost guides you in truth. John 14:17; Even the spirit of truth; whom the world cannot receive, because it seeth him not, neither knoweth him, but ye know him; for he dwelleth with you and shall be in you. The sister I told you about earlier that had the spirit of anger and hatred attack her in church, said when she went home on that Sunday morning, after the enemy attack she told the Lord, "If it was me hindering Pastor this morning, please forgive me." She said that the Holy Ghost immediately spoke back into her spirit and said what do you mean, if? Of course, you were. Even if we don't necessarily want to hear the truth, if we ask, the Holy Ghost will ALWAYS tell us the truth. He will always guide us in the right direction if we will listen.

God did not send us the Holy Ghost just for a feel good, run the isles, shout on Sunday. He sent us the Holy Ghost for power over the enemy. To give us power to tread on serpents and scorpions. Against the evilness of the world. Mark 13:22 tells us; For false Christ's and false prophets shall rise, and shall shew signs and wonders, to seduce, if (it were) possible, even the elect. So, God has equipped his church with power to stand when all of hell is breaking loose. Unfortunately, a lot of the church world today has turned the power of God into nothing more than goose bumps and a feel-good shout. Prophesying pink Cadillac's and good health. The Holy Ghost wasn't sent to help some build themselves a big reputation for faith healing and prosperity. God sent him to protect his church. So, we can stand in perilous and evil times. So that we would have a warrior inside of us, to fight for us. To know the fullness of who God is. To bear fruit that the world can see and be saved. To bear witness to God and say look at him, not look at me. If all you want is a feel-good moment, then all you will have is an occasional goose bump. But if you want the fullness of God, if you want victory in your life and over your enemy, you must sell out totally to him and surrender your all. If you are walking with God in Spirit and in truth, the enemy has no power over you.

WHAT IS THE PURPOSE OF THE
GIFTS OF THE SPIRIT?

The key to Paul's ministry was signs and wonders. It was the miracles and the healings, the word of wisdom and the word of knowledge that Paul operated in that convinced people that Christianity was true. This is the point that I want to make up front about the gifts of the spirit. The reason for the gifts of the spirit is never to exalt the person, the people, or the church in which they are operating. Anyone who exalts themselves in the gifts or merchandises the gift, is in total complete error according to the New Testament. The purpose of the gifts is to authenticate the gospel. Any gift that God operates a believer in, whether it's healing, miracles, or any other it is to authenticate that; number one, God still speaks today; number two, that he still operates today; and number three, he still minsters through people today the way he did throughout scripture.

The nine gifts of the spirit operate on three different dimensions, and it is important to know what these dimensions are. The first dimension is that of inspiration. The bible tells us that all scripture is given by the inspiration of God and is profitable. The word inspiration is a word translated from the Greek that means to breathe upon something. When you speak of someone expiring, it means that they died, which means their breath left them. To inspire is to breathe into or upon. The holy men of God spoke as they were moved upon by the inspiration of the spirit. So, to move in the gifts is to be inspired.

Next, we have the dimension of revelation. These gifts work in what we call the mind gifts. The gift of wisdom and the gift of knowledge are two gifts that need revelation. One of the Greek words that is used for revelation is *apocalypses,* and it means the unveiling of something that has previously been hidden. The third dimension is power. Power is translated from the Greek word *dunamis.* I want to break these three dimensions down in more detail because we are talking about the operation of the nine gifts and what it takes to operate in all nine of them.

Let's take a look at the dimension of inspiration. We only find it once in the New Testament and that is in 2 Timothy 3:16, where it says, all scripture is given by inspiration of God, and is profitable for doctrine, for reproof, for correction, for instruction in righteousness. It is from a Greek word that means God breathed or it can also be rendered; breathe out. Let's look at not just the written word but let's also look at when a prophet would speak. He would come under what is called divine inspiration, meaning God would breathe life upon him or breathe his anointing upon him. 2 Peter 1:21; the prophecy of old time came not by the will of man; but holy men of God spoke when they were moved by the Holy Spirit. Now that word moved, in the New Testament, is to be taken like; when the ship moved as the wind was blowing into its sails. In other words, the ship moves by the direction that the wind is blowing, and the sail is set. That is the imagery of the Holy Spirit moving upon men who wrote the word. Now we are talking about the bible here, however, we are also talking about the gifts of the spirit. The vocal gifts: prophecy, tongues, and interpretation of tongues, must have God breathing upon you in order to operate in those particular gifts. When a gift operates in you there is a motivating force that doesn't come from the outside, but it comes from the inside. You begin to sense a feeling that you cannot ignore. The Holy Spirit places in you a feeling, an inspiration and you know that you are moving in that direction when you cannot get away from it. For example, in the time that Spirit is using you, there is an inner pressing like a burden that cannot be ignored. It is something that you just know, and you cannot get away from it. You may feel like your heart is about to beat out of your chest.

Number two is the dimension of revelation. It is the Greek word *apocolupsus*, meaning to disclose something concealed. Paul spoke to the church about speaking by revelation in Ephesians 3:3, where he said, how that by revelation he made known unto me the mystery. Also, how believers could speak a revelation, in 1 Corinthians 14:26; How is it then, brethren? When ye come together, every one of you hath a psalm, hath a doctrine, hath a tongue, hath a revelation, hath an interpretation. Let all things be done unto edifying. He is not talking about the last book of the New Testament, the book of revelation, he is talking about something which is hidden, which is concealed and having knowledge supernaturally of that thing that is hidden or concealed. One thing that you never want to do is use a gift if you are not sure it is from God. Sometimes people get puffed up spiritually once they have been used in a gift and they misuse their gift for spiritual manipulation. They can cause church splits because of ignorance in how to use the gifts. They begin to think that they are more spiritual than the pastor or leadership of the church, and if they can't tell the pastor how to run the church, they want to pack up their little group and go somewhere else. This is one reason why some pastors hold back when some people try to operate in the gifts, because there has been so much abuse in the churches. Speaking by revelation is speaking the mysteries of God.

Number three is the dimension of power. Spiritual gifts are designated to demonstrate the power of God in the eyes of unbelievers, and you can see that in 1 Corinthians 14:23-24. Spiritual gifts confirm that the word of God is true. Hebrews 2:4, talks about signs, wonders, miracles, and the gifts of the Holy Spirit that operate according to the will of God. Without a demonstration of the Holy Spirit, Christianity becomes like any other religion. It becomes like Islam, it becomes like Buddhism, it becomes like Hinduism. We would just be a belief system. We would just be a religion that has a particular leader. What makes us different is that God answers our prayers with signs and wonders. And that comes through different operations of the gifts of the spirit.

A misconception of the gifts is that they can only operate in a church service. That is not true. The gifts are not limited to a specific facility or a particular church, because your body is the temple of the Holy Ghost. And because your body is the temple, you take the temple everywhere you go. The Holy Spirit abides within you, so you need to be sensitive to the leading of the spirit, wherever you go.

THE MIND GIFTS

Word of Wisdom
Word of Knowledge
Discernment of Spirits

GIFT OF WISDOM

WE ARE GOING TO BEGIN WITH LOOKING AT WHAT IS KNOWN AS THE mind gifts. The very first gift listed is word of wisdom. There is an absolute necessity if you are going to be used in the gifts to first get the gift of wisdom. The gift of the word of wisdom is one of the revelation or what we call revelatory gifts of the spirit. The gifts that reveal insight. The gifts of word of wisdom, word of knowledge, and discernment of spirits are known as mind gifts. They deal with the mind. They deal with the intellect. With the unveiling of something. Worriers focus on problems, but wisdom focuses on solutions. The whole purpose of the gift of the word of wisdom is to provide a significant solution to a very significant problem. This works not only in the realm of spiritual things, but God has enabled this gift to operate in the realm of the natural world to know how to handle problems that may arise in everyday experiences in our life. A revelation gift can do the following: It can reveal what is secret, it can reveal something that is simply unknown, it can reveal the unknown such as what lies ahead in the future. It reveals the mind of the spirit. For example, Paul talks about, who knows the things of man, save the spirit of man that is in him. But who knows the spirit of God except the spirit of God? The word of wisdom is connected to knowing what the mind of the spirit is in each particular situation. Also, it is significant to note that the definition for wisdom is the ability to judge problems properly and make good decisions bringing about good results. So, the result of the word of wisdom or the outcome of the word of wisdom is the positive outcome in a negative situation. If we go to the wisest man that ever lived, we would go to King Solomon. King Solomon in his day was gifted with a gift of wisdom. Solomon talks about wisdom extensively in the book of Proverbs. Proverbs 1:7; Proverbs 9:10; Psalms 111:10, all begin with, the fear of the Lord is the beginning of wisdom. 1 Kings 3:11-12, Solomon asks God for wisdom above all else. And because he asked for wisdom and not for wealth or fame, God gave him everything including wealth and fame.

Wisdom decisions can guide a person through a crisis. It can also provide answers for life's situations. Let's look at James chapter 3. The bible says that there are two types of wisdom. There is wisdom from above and there is wisdom from beneath. It is talking about heavenly wisdom or supernatural wisdom from God and earthly or carnal wisdom. James 3:13-16 says: Who is a wise man and endued with knowledge among you? Let him shew out of a good conversation his works with meekness of wisdom. But if ye have bitterness, envying, and strife in your hearts, glory not, and lie not against the truth. This wisdom descendeth not from above, but is earthly, sensual, devilish. For where envying and strife is, there is confusion and every evil work. But then verses 17 and 18 say; But the wisdom that is from above is first pure, then peaceable, gentle, and easy to be entreated, full of mercy and good fruits, without partiality, and without hypocrisy. And the fruit of righteousness is sown in peace of them that make peace. Here is the difference in the two. Wisdom from above enables you to take a bad situation, a crisis situation or a situation that people can't solve and solve it through the wisdom of the Holy Spirit. Wisdom however from below, earthly wisdom, is a wisdom that learns how to manipulate people for personal gain. So heavenly wisdom is a heavenly manifestation and earthly wisdom is a manipulation.

What is a good definition of knowing that you are working in the gift of wisdom? Wisdom is to know how. It is actually the ability to know how to carry out a plan or how to carry out an assignment, or how to carry out a purpose. Wisdom is knowing how to apply the scriptures. Knowledge is understanding them. True wisdom draws from knowledge, understanding and experiences. The biblical definition for wisdom is the supernatural revelation with the ability given to the mind concerning God's will and plan at that particular moment.

There are seven things that the gift of wisdom, that is wisdom from above, will do in your life.

1. A word of wisdom can settle religious conflicts. In James 15 when they were confused about the Gentiles being grafted in, James spoke up and said, "Look here's what we're going to do with the Gentiles." They cannot commit fornication and they cannot eat meat that was sacrificed to idols. That is what we are going to require of them. It stopped a split in the early church, because one man had a very great word of wisdom.

2. It can settle business disputes. Luke 16:1-8 is a parable of a steward that was about to get fired because he couldn't collect the money that was owed to his employer. He went out with a word of wisdom to everybody that owed his boss and said, "what do you owe?" As each one told him the amount that they owed, he reduced it. For example, one said, "I owe a hundred," and the steward then reduced the amount to eighty. By reducing the amount owed, it enabled them to pay their bill, and the man kept his job because of it.

3. A word of wisdom can silence critics. In Matthew 17:24-27, they presented a question of paying taxes, they were trying to trap Jesus. They asked, "do you pay taxes?" And Jesus answered give to Caesar what belongs to Caesar and give to God what belongs to God. He settled a dispute with his critics by making that statemen. They expected him to resist paying taxes, and they planned to use that against him, and have him arrested. Jesus knew what they were up to because

he had the word of knowledge, so he was able to stop the critics with a word of wisdom.

4. The word of wisdom can win an argument. In Matthew 12:1-8, they are coming to Jesus, and they are fussing at him for healing on the sabbath day. They say, it's illegal, according to the law for you to work on the sabbath day. Instead of debating the sabbath with them, giving his opinion verses their opinion, he said, "well, it's interesting that I have read where David who was not a priest went in on the sabbath day and asked the priest to eat shew bread from the table of shew bread because he was hungry, and God didn't kill him." And that was in the heart of the law. He silenced them and stopped an argument simply by pointing out something everyone knew but ignored.

5. Word of wisdom can solve a very difficult problem. 1 Kings 3, Solomon solves the problem of who the baby belongs to with a word of wisdom.

6. Word of wisdom can answer difficult questions. Look at John 3, where it says, you must be born again. There are two types of people. There are honest hearted doubters and hard-hearted doubters. Thomas was not hard hearted when he said, "I am not going to believe unless I see the nail prints in his hands." He was honest. He wanted to believe but needed some proof. A hard-hearted doubter is someone who has made up their mind about a particular situation. Nothing short of God hitting them upside the head in the middle of the night is going to make them believe. You can wear yourself out and give every argument you know to a hard-hearted doubter, and they are not going to believe. They are out to kill Christians until they get converted supernaturally. Do not waste your time arguing with argumentative people. The bible makes it very clear not to argue with people over stuff that has no bearing whatsoever.

7. Wisdom can help you to escape the snare of Satan. Several years ago, I received a call very late one night. The call came from someone I knew who had called me for help before. I got out of bed and got dressed, getting ready to go, but as I picked up my car keys, I sensed in my spirit that I should not go. I began to pray and felt very strongly not to go. The thought was persistent that the person who called was safe but that I would not be if I went. I was having a conversation with God in my mind, and I began to get a clear picture that I would be involved in an accident and never make it to the person if I went. I didn't go. If we listen to the voice of God, he will tell us when trouble lies ahead.

There are people who desire to be used in the gifts, but they don't pray and seek God for guidance, and they speak out of their own desire and say God said when God did not say. If somebody comes to you and says I have a word from God for you, your spirit will bear witness if it is from God. If you don't feel a connection in your spirit, you don't have to just blindly follow it. If it doesn't bear witness with you, just smile, and go on. Don't lose sleep over it. In these mind gifts, please be aware that you must know how and when to approach someone. James 1:5-8; If any of you lack wisdom, let him ask of God who gives to all men liberally, and upbraideth not; and it shall be given him. But let him ask in faith, nothing wavering. For he that wavereth is like a wave of the sea driven with the wind and tossed. For let not that man think that he shall receive anything of the Lord. A double minded man is unstable in all his ways. So, wisdom in life, is a very important thing to have, whether a person wants to operate in the gift of the spirit or not. It is to know how. How to deal with children who are rebellious. How to deal with things that happen on your job. How to deal with ministry. How to deal with difficult people. Wisdom tells you when and how to operate in the gifts. It tells you the right timing. God may have given you something about someone, it doesn't mean to run right now and tell them. It has to be in the right time to tell them. A lot of times a word of wisdom will confirm something that you already feel in your spirit, and it becomes a witness to you.

I am going to share just a few instances in my life where I have been given a word of wisdom to show how it works on a daily basis.

1. I needed money for a bill. I was praying and asking God to help me take care of this financial obligation when I sensed an urgency in my spirit, use what you have. While I was trying to figure out what I had that I could use I got a phone call with a request for me to make a wedding cake for someone. I was used to baking and decorating cakes for my family, but I had never constructed a tier cake before. I didn't have a clue how to do that. This was before the days of google. I took the job because I needed the money. Then I said, "Okay Lord, show me how to do this." That night I had a dream with great detail on how to make that cake. When I got up the next morning, I knew exactly what to do. I did it and the people doubled the original price because they were so pleased with it.

2. Another time as I was doing some house cleaning, I got out a play pen that I no longer needed and put it aside to get rid of. Suddenly a thought came into my mind and I was hearing, "keep it for Brother Turner." At that point I thought I must be crazy, why in the world would Brother Turner need a babies play pen? That weekend I went to church and Brother Turner made an announcement. If anyone has any baby furniture that they can donate, we are going to start a nursery for the church. I wasn't crazy after all!

3. When I first started Victory Tabernacle, I didn't have a clue what I needed to do to be a legal church. I was told I needed tax numbers and things that I knew nothing about. I asked some people who I thought would know but had no luck. After praying, I picked up a phone book, went directly to the

number I needed. I called and told them my situation. They answered my questions, sent me information and forms that I needed and in no time, I had the tax numbers that I needed.

In each of these situations the word of wisdom showed me how to do what I didn't know how to do. The gift of the word of wisdom works in your daily life to help you do the things that you need to do. It blesses you daily and allows you at times to bless someone else through its use.

THE GIFT OF THE WORD OF KNOWLEDGE

THE GIFT OF THE WORD OF KNOWLEDGE COOPERATES QUITE extensively with the gift of wisdom. You will discover that in many instances when someone is giving a word of knowledge, there will also be a word of wisdom on how to deal with the situation connected with it. It is not a gift of knowledge but the gift of a word of knowledge. The word of knowledge is to communicate verbally an utterance that comes from the Lord on behalf of someone who needs to hear a particular word of knowledge. This is knowledge that comes into the mind. Knowledge in general, is basically the accumulation of information. This knowledge comes from studying and learning about certain things to understand them. For instance, if you want to work with computers you will study to learn all that you can about computers. However, the gift of the word of knowledge is not of human ability but it is a word given by the Holy Spirit. The difference between just having knowledge and receiving a supernatural word of knowledge is a word that I am going to talk about. It is the word intent. The bible says that the word of God is a discerner of thoughts and the intents of the heart. You can usually tell what a person is thinking by listening to what they are saying. Their thoughts turn into words. One of the things word of knowledge can do is to show you the intent of a person's heart. The intent of what their motive is. A lot of times a word of knowledge is connected with discerning of spirits to determine if something is not right with a person. Have you ever had a feeling about someone, but you may not be sure what it is? You know that something is not quite right with this person, but you can't put your finger on the problem. That borderlines on the discerning of spirits and the word of knowledge. At some point their real intent or their real motive will come out. Word of knowledge discerns intents. There are three intents; there are the intentions of God, the intentions of man, and the intentions of Satan. The intentions of Satan are his battle strategies. So, word of knowledge can expose the battle strategy of the enemy before he goes to battle with you. The intentions of men may be that they want to do something or connect with you for their own reasons, and God says you know what, I'm sending them to you because of this, this, and this. And the intentions of God are to fulfill his purpose on earth in the church and through you. So, you have to know the will of God, the intentions of God, and that comes through prayer, and this is when you can receive a particular word of knowledge. There have been a couple of suggestions as to what some believe the word of knowledge to be. Some think it is a gift of the knowledge of the bible. While it is true that the word of knowledge can help you to understand and get knowledge of the bible, remember that this is a supernatural gift of the word of knowledge and not knowledge in general. Then there are others that say that it is an intellectual gift. In other words, God gives you an intellectual ability, and that is the gift of the word of knowledge. Well, this is also required by the Holy Spirit. It takes him to be able to expand your understanding and your intellectual ability. The Holy Spirit, the bible says in 1 John 2:27, is a teacher and he teaches us all things. The word of knowledge is a supernatural gift, and it is not a natural gift that you develop because of having a good intellect, or a good ability to reason.

Here is an example of the word of knowledge. 2 Kings 6:8-20; The Syrian army was in Syria, secretly preparing an attack on Israel. They were doing it behind closed doors. When they went into Israel, they found that all the Israeli troops had been moved from their military position. The general becomes very angry, and they go back to Syria, and they regroup, and the general says, somebody is sending messages to Israel and warning them and I'm going to find out who it is. Now let's try this again. So, he sends a spy to find out where Israel is camped. The spy goes back to Syria and reports his findings. The general plans a strategy once again to attack Israel. He goes to Israel, into the valley where they were supposed to be, and there is nobody there. This is the second time this has happened, so now the general is suspicious that he has a spy in the camp. He gets angry and confronts his men. The men tell him, "Sir there is not a spy in the camp, but here is the problem. There is a man with a double portion anointing that lives in Israel by the name of Elisha. Every time you go in secret to make a strategy, his God through prayer tells him what your plans are." So now the general decides the easiest way to deal with this problem, is to go capture Israel's prophet. Now this is not a very smart idea, because if the prophet has already discovered that you are coming twice before, do you not think that he is going to know when you plan to show up for the third time. This is how crazy earthly carnal knowledge is. It just doesn't figure the thing out. Obviously if he is a prophet, he is going to figure out that you are coming. So, they do a secret strategy to go to Dothan, which was a big mountain near the Jordan river. And the prophet is there, and he gets up with his servant, and they look and the whole mountain is surrounded with the army of Syria. The servant is not as discerning as the prophet is and he says, "oh, master, what will we do? We are surrounded by the Syrian army?" But Elisha doesn't get rattled. He just kind of looks around and then says, "you just don't see what I see. I need to pray for you to see what I see." The servant's eyes are supernaturally opened, and he sees that the mountain is surrounded by horses with chariots of fire. Can you imagine? God has sent a whole army of angels there to protect them. Then the story begins to get funny, because Elisha goes down to the army, and God blinds the whole Syrian army. Elisha takes the arm of one of the soldiers and leads them right to the Israeli army! The Syrians are no doubt thinking, we are in trouble now. They said we are not doing any wars as long as this prophet is living. This all came about because of a man who was able to pray and to get a word of knowledge from God.

About ninety percent of the time a word of knowledge is to lift you up out of a despondency or to encourage you in a direction that you are going. The gifts are for edification. To build up. The mind gifts are dealing with your mind. Meaning God gives you a word of wisdom because there is something that you need to know 'how to'. Then he gives you a word of knowledge because you are battling and you need encouragement, you need direction. If you are given a word of knowledge for someone else, don't forget the mind gifts are dealing with the mind of that person, about something that they need to know. The word of knowledge can also be for the body. The church can be going through something. There can be a situation going on that is affecting the entire body or the mental thinking of the entire congregation.

In 1 Kings chapter 14 there was a prophet name Ahijah. Jeroboam the king has a son who is sick, and Jeroboam wants to enquire of a prophet whether his son will live or die. There was a prophet living in Shiloh. The king does not want to go because everyone will know him. So, he sends his wife, and he says here is what I want you to do, "I don't want anybody to know that you are going so I want you to disguise yourself." Now here is the thing that is amazing. The prophet had never been informed that the kings' wife was coming. And the prophet is totally blind. This is an absolute example of the gift of the word of knowledge. The blind prophet could not see but before she ever got to his house, he got a divine word of knowledge that the king's wife was coming to enquire about her son. Now imagine this. The king's wife is standing at the door, her identity disguised, and the prophet says, "come in thy wife of Jeroboam." You can't hide anything from God. God told him who was coming, how she was coming (disguised), and what she was coming about.

Let me share a personal example of this gift in my own life. An acquaintance of mine came to visit one day and brought a friend with her. The friend appeared to be another woman. The friend looked like a woman, dressed like a woman, and sounded like a woman. But in my spirit, I kept hearing, this is a man. Finally, I asked the lady that had brought this person to go into the other room with me and I asked directly, "why are you trying to pass a man off as woman?" She looked at me with a shocked look and said, "how did you know?" He fools everybody. I told her they might fool people, but never would they fool God. God will show you when someone is trying to deceive you if you will be sensitive to the spirit and listen.

Why is the gift of the word of knowledge and prophecy so powerful? 1 Corinthians 14:25 says: thus are the secrets of their hearts manifest. It will cause unbelievers to fall down and worship God and say of a truth God is among you. In other words, the gift of the word of knowledge is given at times not only to help encourage you, but a word of knowledge can be given at times to reveal something so that people will know that God can know and speak to them about a situation that no one else knows about. The Lord knows what I'm going through. The Lord knows about these people I've been dealing with, and nobody knew except God that I was dealing with this issue.

The bible is full of examples of the word of knowledge being used. You can have the gift of knowledge and still not know everything about people. There are times when God shows you and there are times when he hides things from you. Look at Elisha. When his servant Gehazi ran after Naaman and took gifts from him, Elisha knew about it even though Gehazi lied. But then when the Shunamite woman came to him because her son had died, Elisha told Gehazi to leave her alone because he knew something was wrong, but he said, "the Lord has hidden it from me." There are some people who operate very heavily in the gift of the word of knowledge. They can call people out and tell them things and be right on. But God does not always allow everything to be known. It is according to the sovereign plan of God. Some things need to be known to accomplish or build up the kingdom of God while some things should not be known. It is up to the Lord himself to determine the level of what he wants to operate that gift in or how he wants to use that gift to edify the body of Christ.

The is more than one use or purpose of the word of knowledge. One purpose of the word of knowledge is to reveal secrets as a sign to the unbeliever. 1 Corinthians 14:25; thus, the secrets of the flesh are made manifest, and he will fall down on his face and worship God saying, I know that God is among you. Another purpose for this gift is to warn of coming judgment. In Sodom and Gomorrah, Genesis 18:17-18, God said, "shall I hide this thing from Abraham." In Amos it says that God doeth nothing except he reveals it to his prophets. In Jonah 3:4, Nineveh was warned for forty days to repent, or they would experience utter destruction. Christ warned of the destruction that was going to come to Jerusalem and that it would come on that generation. In Numbers chapter 3, the word of knowledge is used to expose a dangerous sin. Joshua was given a word in Joshua 1:19 that the Lord would be with him wheresoever he went. They conquered Jericho and then they go to a city called Ai. It is a small city, so they just send a portion of the army in, and they are defeated. So, Joshua says hold on here, God we have a problem, what am I to do now. We utterly wiped-out Jericho, did everything you said there, now we go into this little city and get defeated. How am I going to get these people to fight now, after I told them that you are with us and that we could win victories. In Joshua 7:10, the Lord said to Joshua, "Get thee up; wherefore liest thou upon thy face." You have one man that totally did the opposite of what I said. I said everything was to come into the treasury, but you have a guy from the tribe of Judah by the name of Achan, and he has kept back garments that he has hidden, and I am not going to bless you because you didn't give everything. When confronted Achan confessed what he had done. Therefore, Joshua knew through a word of knowledge, "this is what's wrong, this is who did it, and this is how you are to deal with it." After that, they took the other thirty cities with no problem.

Before God exposes a sin, whether it be in a person or in the body of Christ, he will warn them of coming judgment.

1. God will always visit in mercy before he visits in judgment. Exodus 33:19; And he said, I will make all my goodness pass before thee, and I will proclaim the name of the Lord before thee; and will be gracious to whom I will be gracious and will show mercy on whom I will show mercy. God doesn't just see something and instantly judge it. He is patient, longsuffering, he is not willing for people to perish. But sometimes people get to a place where they will no longer repent. They no longer say God help me. God I'm sorry. When they quit doing that then judgment can come.

2. God always gives a space to repent before judgment comes. Revelation 2:21; And I gave her space to repent of her fornication; and she repented not.

3. God will rescue the righteous before a national judgment cycle. In 2 Peter 2:9, talking about Lot and Sodom where it says God knows how to deliver the Godly and to reserve the righteous to the day of judgment.

The word of Knowledge can come as a sign to the unbeliever, warning of a coming judgment, to warn and to expose a dangerous sin, and to forewarn of satanic setups. The Lord has forewarned me on a couple of different occasions that someone was coming into the church to cause harm. On one of these occasions, I had a dream three nights in a row where I was sitting in the back seat of a car with one of my brothers who was deceased, and a man and woman got into the front seat. Each time my brother looked at me and said, watch out for these two. Don't let them drive because they mean to do you harm. A week or two later a man and woman walked into the church, and I instantly felt in my spirit that they were the two I had seen in my dream. They told me that he was a minister and that they were looking for a church where they could work and be a help. They immediately began to try to get control of different ministries in the church and were working behind my back to influence some of the congregation against me. It ended with the man asking in front of the church at a business meeting how anyone went about getting rid of the pastor. Since I had been warned and was on my guard during all of this, I was not taken by surprise. I told him the steps that had to be taken to get me out and then informed him that if he managed to get through all those steps, he would still have to get past God and his plans for this church. Needless to say, their plan failed, and they moved on. This is just a demonstration of how God prepares us and warns us of coming danger through a word of knowledge.

When you are used in the gifts you must be careful not to get into a habit of saying, "God said," when maybe it's just something that you are sensing in yourself and not necessarily God speaking to you. It's just something you feel in your spirit. Sometimes it can be the discerning of spirits, not to be spoken, but for your own knowledge. Scripture tells us to try the spirit to see if it is of God. So, in other words it may not always be the Lord talking to you. Look at Peter. Jesus asked who do men say that I am. Peter said thou art the Christ the son of the living God. And Jesus says, "flesh and blood hath not revealed this to you but the Father which is in heaven." Now Peter is all excited and thinking, woohoo, I got a word from God. God spoke to me. A couple of verses later, Jesus is telling everybody he is going to die, and Peter said be it far from you Lord. Now Peter is thinking he has gotten another revelation, but Jesus turns and rebukes him. He says, "get thee hence Satan." So here one minute Peter is getting a word from God and the next minute the devil is after him. This is the life of a church member. This is the only way you can explain people that were great church members, they loved God and the church, but next thing you know they are mad at everybody, talking about everybody, and you are wondering what happened. It is because if you are not careful you can let circumstances take you from spiritual to carnal in the blink of an eye. You can also go from being in the flesh and suddenly, God begins speaking to you. Always be careful how you share something when you think it is God giving you a word of wisdom or a word of knowledge. Instead of saying, "the Lord told me something about you," it is better to say, "you know, I felt something in my spirit, and you judge it." If they say something in the affirmative like, "Oh, I have been praying about that." Then it is a word from the Lord. Let them determine whether or not they think it is a word from the Lord. If it was from God and they just refuse to accept it, then you have still done your part and your conscience is clear, and it is up to them what they do with it. If God gives you a word of knowledge about someone that you think is having a problem. Don't tell them before you pray about it. You may be wrong in your perception, and you can embarrass that person, embarrass yourself and you can hurt their reputation. There have been people put God's name in the middle of gossip and cause church hurts and church splits. If you operate in a cautious and sensitive manner, it will only add to your credibility when you speak. You don't have to go around saying that you are a prophet or that the Lord talks to you. Your reputation will tell what you are.

DISCERNING OF SPIRITS

THIS GIFT IS OFTEN CALLED THE GIFT OF DISCERNMENT, BUT THAT is an incorrect term. It is discerning of Spirits. It is important to understand that the gift here concerns spirits and not just discernment or discerning. The word used for discernment here is translated from the Greek word *deocresees* and it means a judicial judgment. A judicial judgment by weighing the evidence. The idea is to have the ability to determine or judge the presence or the activity of a particular type of spirit. Now before we talk about discerning of spirits and is not the discerning of a spirit (singular) but of spirits (plural), meaning different types of spirits, let us look at why it is necessary. There are seven reasons why discerning of spirits is necessary or in general why the ability to discern things is significant.

1. The gift is used to determine what is of the flesh and what is of the spirit. An example of this is when James and John, as they were walking through Samaria with Jesus, wanted to call fire down on them because they rejected him. But Jesus said, "you don't know what manner of spirit you are of." This is not from me. This is of your flesh. This is something your fleshly man wants to do. So, we must determine the difference between spirit and flesh.

2. To determine if the spirit is from God or if it's from the enemy. For example, 1 Samuel 28, a witch with a familiar spirit conjures up what appears to be Samuel, Saul is there

but he never sees this person, he only has the witch's word for it. Saul never really hears what he says, the witch is speaking her voice out of what the spirit is saying. There are some who suggest that she actually conjured up the spirit of the righteous man Samuel, in the presence of King Saul. It is more likely that she was imitating a spirit in order to fool Saul. There are several reasons why you can see why that was. For one God would not answer Saul by the Holy Spirit, and there was no other known method of that day in which God would speak to people, so he went to a witch with a familiar spirit which was forbidden by the law of Moses and consulted her. God is not going to speak or bring a righteous man back through demonic activity. So, you must determine what is from the spirit of God and what is not from the spirit of God.

3. It helps us to determine what type of spirit we are dealing with. Jesus saw a woman bowed over. People might look at her and say, she has crippling arthritis, or maybe she has a birth defect in her back. Jesus called it a spirit of infirmity. He detected by discerning of spirits that this was not a normal physical ailment. It was not a normal back problem. It was a spirit of infirmity that had to be removed from her body.

4. The spirit of discernment is used to tell if a person is vexed, oppressed, or possessed of a devil. It is important to understand there are three ways a spirit can attack a person. Vexation, when someone says I feel vexed in my spirit, it is a pressure that you feel. A weight and a heaviness that you feel. Oppression, or when a person is oppressed, they cannot think clearly, nor can they focus clearly, and they can become very depressed once they become oppressed. Possession is total control. When a person is possessed, they have no power of their own to resist that spirit. The man in Mark 5, who was possessed with demons was cutting

himself with stones, it was actually a suicide spirit, because we learn later that when Jesus sent the spirits into the pigs, they ran off the cliff and drowned themselves. The suicide spirit that was affecting this man was causing him to cut himself with stones. He's crying day and night because he is tortured and tormented. Anytime a person is dealing with a demon, you must discern which it is, the vexation, the oppression, or the possession. You don't try to cast a spirit out of someone that is just vexed by an enemy. Rebuke the enemy. When they are oppressed by the enemy, sometimes all they need is a refreshing of the Holy Spirit to renew their mind. With a possessed person, it's a whole other thing. When a real demon shows up you will know it. They can speak in different voices from the person they are possessing. They cause that person to have a supernatural strength. Remember in Acts chapter 19 about the seven sons of Sceva? They tried to cast the devil out of a man and the devil spoke and said Jesus I know, and Paul I know but who are you? Then the one possessed jumped the seven sons of Sceva and they left that house naked and bruised. It is a real serious issue. When someone is possessed, the demon has to be expelled or cast out by the power of the name of Jesus. But vexation, oppression and depression are not dealt with by commanding a demon to come out of that person because the vexation or oppression is in the mind. It comes through prayer and praying something to the effect of, "God free her or him now from this and bring in the spirit to refresh in the name of Jesus." That's where discernment comes in to show you the difference in vexation, oppression, and possession.

5. It is to determine the method with which to deal with the spirit. 1 Corinthians 12:6 tells us that there are diversities of operation, but it is the same God which worketh. How do you deal with a particular spirit? There must be a method with which you deal with it. Sometimes it's through prayer,

sometimes it's through resisting, sometimes it's through rebuking.

6. To determine if an angel is from God or from the enemy. Galatians 1:8 teaches us that someone can come into the church teaching something other than the true gospel or an angel from heaven can come teaching another gospel. There are two religious groups totally based on an alleged angelic visitation. One of them is Islam which is based on Gabriel coming to Mohamed giving him a revelation. The only problem with that Muslim revelation is that when Gabriel came to Mohamed he said, Jesus is not the son of God. But when Gabriel came to Mary, he said, Jesus is the Son of God. So, the problem there is what? The angel. One was from God, and one obviously wasn't. The other religion is Mormonism. Mormonism according to Joseph Smith was that an angel showed him these gold plates, and he translated them looking through two stones. If you know the Mormon religion, you know it teaches contrary to the doctrine of the New Testament. Maybe he saw an angel, maybe he didn't. Maybe he made up a story, but if he saw an angel, and it is contrary to the gospel that was taught by the apostles. What does Galatians 1:8 say? Let them be accursed. So, we must determine if an angel messenger is from the Lord or if it is the enemy trying to deceive you.

7. Hebrews 4:12, the discerning of spirits is able to determine the thoughts and intents of the heart, and this is done by the presence of the Holy Spirit. Now once again, notice that it is discerning of spirits. So, let's talk about the four different types of spirits that are involved in the gift of discerning of spirits.

FOUR TYPES OF DISCERNING OF SPIRITS.

1. First, as strange as it may sound it is to determine the presence of God. Or the presence of the Spirit of God. In Genesis chapter 28 verse 16, Jacob saw a ladder with angels descending up and down and he said the Lord was in this place and I knew it not. In other words, it was God's presence that was there, and he didn't discern what it was. Then we find in John chapter 12 and verse 29, people began to hear a voice from heaven, and it says some people said it thundered and others said it was an angel that spoke to Christ. Now it was God's voice, but the higher level of spiritual people said that's the voice of God, while other's that were not quite on the same spiritual level said that must have been an angel and others said, did you all hear that thunder? Some were so out of tune spiritually that they could not discern what the actual voice was. What we see today are that too many people are quick to say what is and what is not of God. When people disagree with something a preacher or another Christian says, they want to cry out, they are not of God, this is not of God, that music is not of God. In reality what they are doing is, they have a particular preference or style they like and anything that is outside of their preference, is not of God. People get so caught up in their tradition and their preference that they make it of God or not of God based on what they feel God likes. They are not really basing it upon what God actually likes or dislikes, they are basing it upon their own personal likes and dislikes. So, this is why discerning of spirits of what is of God and what is not of God is so important. Because you must separate if from your tradition, you must separate it from what your personal preference is and go into the scripture and look at it from a biblical perspective.

2. Satan is an angel, so you must discern satanic spirits. You must discern the presence of Satan. Jesus encountered Satan for forty days and Paul may have also encountered him at times in the form of a hindering spirit. Ephesians 6:2 says we wrestle not against flesh and blood but against principalities, powers, rulers of the darkness, wicked spirits in heavenly places. Luke chapter 13 indicates that there was a woman who was bowed over by a spirit of infirmity, and the spirit had to be cast out before the woman's body could be completely healed. We discover in Acts 16:16-18 that there was a woman with a fortune telling spirit that was following Paul and Silas saying, "these men are the servants of the most high God." Paul knew that even though what she was saying was true it wasn't a right spirit. When he got grieved the anointing came on him and he rebuked it and the fortune telling woman lost all of her powers to be able to tell the future. So, it is important that we discern spirits, that we can discern demonic activity or demonic spirits. When you are a Christian, your spirit will bear witness of other Christians but when you encounter someone who is not a child of God, then your spirit will clash with that spirit that is in them.

3. We must know how to discern the spirit in men. We are a body, a soul, and a spirit. You can watch a person's physical actions or body language when you are talking to them and know if they are really paying attention to you. If they are on their phone or looking away, they are not paying attention to you. You can tell sometimes how people stand if they are in a hurry or not in a hurry. You can tell by the eyes. If people are lying, they don't like to make eye contact with you. Men have a spirit within them. An inner spirit. The discernment of spirits will let you learn how to read or detect what a person is thinking on the inside of their spirit. Look at times throughout the ministry of Jesus, that there

were times that he knew their thought. Was he reading their minds? No. He was determining what was really going on in their spirit. Hebrews 4:12 says, the word of God is quick and powerful, and it can discern thoughts and intents of the heart. You can read peoples body language, but you can't always read the intent of their heart. They can hide that. They can look at you and say Hi, while their heart is saying hurry up and get out of my way. The real discerning of spirits can look at someone who is looking at you smiling and the Holy Spirit will say there is something wrong with that. That is not right. When we talk about discerning the intents of someone it comes from two Greek word *en* which is **in** and *naose* which is **mind**. It means what is in the mind. The intents of the heart are those things which are hidden, or so people think, and the Holy Spirit enables you to discern them out.

4. Another type of spirit that we need to discern is angelic spirits. Because in the bible God makes his angels spirits. In Hebrews 1:14 and Hebrews 13:2 are some verses that say we can entertain angels unaware. We see them as strangers, and we are unaware that they are angels. Meaning people that come and look like they are in a human form could actually be a messenger of God. In Genesis chapters 18 and 19 two angels came down to Lot before the destruction of Sodom and Gomorrah. These were angels that looked like men. In Psalms 104:4 it says he makes his angels spirits; he makes his ministers a flaming fire. We know they appear in the form of men. In Joshua chapter 5 there was an angel that stood at the edge of the camp, and he was called the captain of the Lord's host. The Hebrew word for host means armies. It refers to angelic armies. We need discernment to discern first the spirit of God. We don't want to ever say the Lord showed up, but we didn't recognize him. And we don't want to call something not of God just because we differ with a

preference or a style. Or if we disagree on theology with someone. The second thing is to discern Satan or demonic activity. The third is to discern the intent of people. Because you don't want to deal with someone that looks good, and the Holy Spirit is saying there is something not right about them. Their heart, their motive is not right. The fourth one is the presence of the angels of the Lord.

DISCERNING OF EVIL SPIRITS OR DEMONS.

We have talked about discerning Satan and demonic spirits. We should add a fifth category here of discerning demons, or demon spirits. Demons are spirit beings, and we need to be able to recognize the enemy. In the bible you have foul spirits, unclean spirits, evil spirits, seducing spirits. In the New Testament, these evil spirits, if you look at the word that is commonly used, we would call it a demon. It is a spirit that is evil. Its ultimate goal is to possess an individual, meaning to take total control of them. Satan comes to steal, to kill and to destroy. Certain sicknesses, certain infirmities in the bible were caused by a demonic possession of that person. There are numerous types of demons mentioned in the bible. Let me name a few of the demon spirits talked about in the bible.

1. 1 Kings 22:23 there is a lying spirit. It is only mentioned one time in the bible, but it is easy to see that, that spirit is released all over America.

2. Leviticus 20:6 a familiar spirit. A familiar spirit is a spirit that works very heavily in the occult. In other words, if you know someone that is into seances, palm reading or tarot card reading, it would be done by a familiar spirit, which is strictly forbidden in several places in God's law in the Torah. A familiar spirit will also lead people into deception. It will tell people things and cause them to react based on what

they've heard, and a lot of times bring them into terrible problems and situations.

3. Deuteronomy 18:19 a spirit of divination. The spirit of divination is what we would call today fortune telling. Anyone who is involved in tarot card reading, palm reading, or in astrology reading of the stars and that type of thing would be someone that could be connected to a spirit of divination or a familiar spirit.

4. Numbers 5:14 the spirit of jealousy. Now Numbers 5 deals with the concept that if a husband believes that his wife has committed adultery she had to go through a very bizarre test, called the trial of bitter waters. If she was guilty her stomach would swell and if she was not guilty her stomach would not swell. And this is how he would know. A spirit of jealousy is extremely powerful and is very strong. It can cause people to kill other people. Saul was so jealous of David that he tried on several occasions to kill him.

5. Romans 8:15 the spirit of bondage. This is a spirit that brings a person back into sin. Back into spiritual bondage, spiritual captivity.

6. Luke 13:11 the spirit of infirmity, which is a spirit of weakness, of total physical weakness.

7. 2 Timothy 1:7 a spirit of fear. We all have experienced some type of fear. There is a positive fear, such as I won't step out in the road with traffic because I might get run over or I won't stick my hand in the fire because I will get burned. There is a fear that people can have that can keep them from danger. But a spirit of fear that is not good is one that brings torment. You know it is a spirit of fear when you become tormented and obsessed by it. You can't sleep at night, you can't rest, you have moved beyond a normal fear into a spirit of fear.

8. 1 Timothy 4:1 a spirit of seduction. Some shall depart from the faith, giving heed to seducing spirits. Most of the

time people think when you say a spirit of seduction you are talking about a sexual spirit. While it can be that it is generally a spirit that pulls people away from the truth. It's something that comes on a person to blind them, and they will go into sin because they are deceived and they can't see that what they are doing is wrong.

9. Mark 9:25 a spirit of deafness. When Jesus rebuked the deaf and dumb spirit and the spirit came out of the person, that person was able to hear completely.

10. Acts 16:16 a spirit of python. The spirit of python is the fortune telling spirit and when you look up that this woman had the spirit of divination, and you check what that word means it is actually called the spirit of python. It wants power and control. It wants to be seen and heard. It most generally will attack the leadership to get control.

11. 1 John 4:3 a spirit of antichrist. This spirit is mentioned four times in first, second and third John. A spirit of antichrist according to John's epistle is the spirit that denies the relationship between, God the father and his son Jesus. A spirit that denies that Jesus is the son of God.

12. Mark 5:2 an unclean spirit. In Mark 9:25 it is called a foul spirit.

Before we get into what the discernment of spirits is, let's look at what it is not. Sometimes to better understand what something is, you need to understand what it is not. What the gift of discernment is not. It is not the gift of suspicion. If someone is a person of interest in a crime they come under suspicion. The law enforcement thinks they are guilty when they become a suspect. Often people see faults in others and claim that they have discerned something but many times they are actually fault finding. The bible talks about backbiters, gossipers, and tale bearers. Anyone that has that type of spirit on them, has a tendency of trying to find the worst in a person, the worst in a situation, any gossip they can find out about someone that they don't particularly like. Some people are under a gift of suspicion, and they are classifying it as a spirit of discernment. The problem is that what you perceive to be fact may not actually be fact. Perry Stone told a story about his father when he was a young evangelist, being in revival. The revival was going great but right after the revival started, he took his younger sister with him to visit another one of his sisters that was in the hospital. When he went to church that night, the people had turned cold. He went back the next night, and it was still a cold atmosphere. He's praying Lord, what went wrong? So, the pastor comes to him and tells him that one of the men in the church had seen him going into the hospital with a strange woman. He said they were hidden under an umbrella, and it just didn't look right. The pastor told him that what he needed to do was publicly explain what he did and his error to the church and make it right. So, Brother Stone said I will be glad to do that. So, he first explains to the pastor that he had taken his younger sister with him to the hospital to visit the other sister. He said it was raining so I was holding an umbrella over her and had my arm around her because I didn't want her to fall. The pastors face turned red. The next night Brother Stone addressed the church. He brought his sister with him, had her stand up and explained what had happened. He openly rebuked the church and the man for their gossip. But one man's suspicions and gift of gab, halted a revival that God had ordained.

The gift of discernment is not the gift of speculation. Speculation is forming a theory of conjecture without firm evidence. Most rumors are founded on speculation. When someone says the Lord told me something was going to happen and it don't happen, it was speculation. The gift of discernment of spirits has nothing to do with speculation.

The gift of discerning of spirits has nothing to do with information. People get information from other people or social media and try to make others think that they have received a discerning of a spirit. They collect information and then they say,

God told me. Don't ever take information that you have gotten from another source and tie the name of God to it and act like God showed you something. The gift of discernment is a supernatural gift that enables a person to judge and detect spirits, all of the four different types of spirits that we have talked about.

Discerning of spirits can work in cooperation with the gifts of word of wisdom and word of knowledge. Mark 2:6-8 says, but there were certain of the scribes sitting there and reasoning in their hearts, why does this man speak blasphemy. Who can forgive sins but God? And immediately, Jesus perceived in his spirit, that they so reasoned within themselves. So, he said to them, why reason these things in your heart? Now the perception of what Christ perceived was in his spirit and not from his mind. The gift of discerning of spirits, works through the Holy Spirit that dwells in your spirit. How does this gift operate? Let's look at some examples: In John 1:47, Jesus said to Nathaniel behold an Israelite in whom there is no guile. I saw you sitting under the tree. There was nobody there to see him sitting under the tree and yet Christ saw him. So, Christ had a word of knowledge that he knew from Nathaniel, that in him there was no guile. That is the discerning of a man's spirit.; Mark 2:8, Jesus said to the Pharisees that he perceived in his spirit that they had reasoned among themselves, now he is discerning the negative attitude coming out of the Pharisees.; Matthew 16:8, Jesus says to his disciples, oh ye of little faith. The gift of discerning of spirits, can discern faith level or the unbelief in the atmosphere coming out of the spirits and hearts of people.; Matthew 22:18, Jesus said to the leaders he perceived their wickedness. Now all of these scriptures talk about, he perceived. In Luke 5:22 where Jesus is addressing the Pharisees, Jesus perceived their thoughts and said why do you reason this in your heart. Luke chapter 20:23, Jesus again speaking to the Pharisees this, when Jesus perceived their craftiness, he said, "why tempt ye me?" Now there is one word that keeps coming up and you heard it – he perceived, he perceived, he perceived. We could translate it this way, he discerned, he discerned, he discerned. Because this is the gift of discerning of spirits. He's not discerning demons, he is discerning the heart, the thoughts, the intents and what's coming from their heart, and spirit, and mind. So, when he perceived, it means he discerned it, he detected it. These are good examples because it is coming from the ministry of Jesus, and it shows how the gift operates. The word perceive is to know. It's an inner knowledge, it's not just the existence of some pre-known knowledge that a person is acting upon. The five senses are always used when it comes to the gift of discerning. Hebrews 5:14, But strong meat belongeth to them that are of full age, even those who by reason of use have their senses exercised to discern both good and evil.

And so, we must have discerning of spirits. Why? Number one is to discern false prophets. You must keep false prophets out of the church through discerning of spirits. Number two, you must keep evil out of the church with the discerning of spirits. There are those who have pedophile spirits, there are those that have sexual spirits on them. And when they come into a congregation where there are a lot of young people or someone catches their attention, you need the gift of discernment of spirits to recognize those spirits. You must keep the proper people involved in the working of the ministry. If their motives are wrong, it can cause great problems. That is why you see news reports where young people have been abused by someone in the church. Whether it's a priest, a youth minister, or a Sunday School teacher. You must know their spirit. You must have discerning of spirits, not suspicion to recognize these things. It makes it much easier to protect yourself, your church, and your people.

God will often give those of you who are in ministry and those of you that have a special anointing for ministry, an ability to discern certain things. One man from the great healing revivals years ago could discern the type of spirit by taking a person's hand. He could just hold their hand and pray, and the Lord would reveal to him the spirit that he was dealing with, and he would know what he was praying against. When he prayed things happened.

The gift of the discerning of spirits can also be used to detect the atmospheres. In Nazareth there was an atmosphere of unbelief. Some of the cities like Capernaum, Corizeme, Magdala, places where Jesus ministered, he upbraided them because of their unbelief. Other places where Jesus would minister, some of the places where the Gentiles were, you would see greater results. Because by the discerning of spirits, Jesus could tell whether or not the individuals were ready spiritually to hear the word, ready spiritually for ministry. And this happens today.

Now what can be discerned? What truly is from the Lord and what truly is not from the Lord. Remember again to watch your personal preferences, so that you are not judging something saying you are discerning it when you personally just don't like it. Discerning of spirits will show you when a person's motive is right or wrong. When a person is bound by an unclean spirit, we need the discerning of spirits to be able to tell that this person doesn't just have a problem, but they are being tortured by a spirit. You can usually tell, after years of experience in the ministry, by looking very carefully into people's eyes. You can see that they are being tortured, they are being tormented, that there is something that has got them bound up. The eyes are a gateway into their spirit as to what is bothering them. That is just an interesting thought. There is no bible verse that says look into their eyes, other than Jesus said the light of the body is the eyes.

When a person has an unclean or evil intent, it is very important to have the discerning of spirits. It lets you know when someone is up to no good. You may not know exactly what they are up to, but you know that something doesn't feel right, and it puts you on your guard.

In receiving this gift, there are three things I want to tell you. First of all, every gift including this one must be prayed for. God help me to have more discernment. Help me to have discerning of spirits. Help to know what I need to know to keep trouble at bay and to protect myself against enemy strategies. Now when you pray for this gift you need to be careful to recognize when you begin to know things about people supernaturally, what to do with it. If you are an extra sensitive personality, sensitive to spiritual things, the enemy may try to get you to use the gift in a wrong way. It is not given for the purpose of gossip. It is not given to make you judgmental or critical. Perry Stone said he had someone tell him once that they had been called to go to different ministries to expose the problem the ministry was having and make it public. He said he thought to himself, no you came because you like to gossip, and it proved itself to be true. They were simply a gossip and they loved to talk to make themselves feel more important. When you pick up on things, just remember that you must have great discernment, making sure that what you are seeing, or hearing is not just the enemy giving you a thought. Remember when Peter said to Jesus, you will not die? It was the enemy, not God telling him that. The second thing is to remember that good people operating in gifts, can sometimes get off track. In fact, people that are operating very heavily in a gift must guard themselves from getting off track. This gift must be mixed with wisdom or great damage could be done. It must be used with wisdom on how you talk to people and how you minister. The Third thing is that sometimes God will show you something and it is not meant to be made public. Some things are meant for you to pray about. If you feel like the Lord shows you something that you need to share with someone and the person says, I don't see that, don't get offended and puffed up. If you do, God will stop using you. You must operate in the right spirit. The gift of discernment can expose the attack plan of the enemy. It can cut off the attack before it occurs because you have been made aware of it and have your guard up. It can give you advanced understanding in a situation. The spirit of discernment is a necessity in the day and time that we are living in.

THE POWER GIFTS

Working of Miracles
Gift of Healing
Gift of Faith

WORKING OF MIRACLES

The working of miracles is the fifth gift mentioned in 1 Corinthians 12:10. Let me introduce this by saying that Christianity is different than any other known religion in the world for this reason. Every other religion, whether it be Islam, Buddhism, or Hinduism they all had a teacher. Whether it be Buddha or Muhammad or some other individual, they were considered to be inspired teachers. Some considered their teachers to be prophets. They all have their own books, just as Christians have the Bible. The Muslims have the Koran, the Hindus and Buddhist also have their own books. Which are the writings handed down by their leader or by the teachers that were involved with that particular leader. All of them have a particular belief system, of how they are connected to God. What makes Christianity absolutely different and what has made Christianity different for over the past nineteen hundred and eighty some years is the gift of miracles. Christianity is the only religion that produces results from the God of heaven and from His son Jesus Christ. Other religions pray for miracles, and they just don't see miracles. Now there are satanic counterfeit miracles, we know that. Jannes and Jambrese in the book of Exodus counterfeited a miracle that Aaron did. Remember when Aaron through down his rod and it turned into a snake? Then Jannes and Jambrese threw down their rod and it also became a snake. But don't forget Aaron's rod swallowed their rod. God still came through. The Egyptian magicians even began to counterfeit several of the miracles that

God was doing which is quite humorous, because there are plagues everywhere and they only added more plagues by imitating God's original. The one thing that they could not do according to the book of Exodus was to undo the original miracles that God performed. In line with that, we can say that Christianity is different because of the miraculous occurrences manifested by God through his people.

Having said all of that, let me go on and say that there is not a season or day of miracles. There is only a God who continually works miracles. Everything about Christianity is based upon the miraculous. The creation is a miraculous event. Opening the barren wombs of women that were too old to have children, was and is miraculous. The exodus is filled with miracles. The prophets worked miracles. Christ and the apostles and His followers worked miracles. We see God as a miracle working God.

What is the definition of a miracle? The definition of a miracle is this: divine intervention, to alter a situation that man is unable to change without God's help. In the New Testament Greek there is not a particular word used for miracle. The English word miracle comes from the Latin word *miraculum*, which refers to something that evokes wonder or amazement to people. However, there are four primary words in the New Testament that are used when the miraculous occurs. These four words are the word *zimieiln* which means a sign, evidence of a divine act occurring, authenticating the message of the gospel and the working of God's presence. We then have the Greek word *terrus* which means a wonder. We have a Greek word that is often translated as the word power throughout the New Testament, and that word is *dunamus*. Then we have the Greek word, *alguun* which means work, labor, action, and deed. It is interesting to note that these four words do not depict different types of miracles. They are words that are connected to a miraculous event which happened and often are connected with the reaction, the amazement or the wonder or just the work itself, that God did relate to that particular deed or that particular miracle. A true miracle that comes from God, cannot be explained away, or credited to natural phenomenal or human logic.

Now I want to give some general information. Some of this information might be debatable in how a person counts a miracle, or what a person considers to be a miracle. I am going to try to give a foundational study on the miraculous. The Bible itself has one hundred and twenty-four miracles that is said to be recorded in it, including the creation story, the flood story, and the fall of the tower of babel. The four gospels credit about three dozen miracles with Jesus. In fact, some count about thirty-seven in all. In the book of Acts for example, if we include the miracle of tongues at Pentecost, there are about nineteen miracles listed just in the book of Acts. Six were done by Peter, nine were done by Paul, the others were done by other individuals. So, we see from Genesis all the way through to the end of our New Testament book of Revelation, that the Bible as a whole is a miraculous book filled with stories that are involved with our God performing something that was impossible for man to do, without His divine intervention.

Now some miracles were performed by God Himself. Two such examples would be the creation and the plagues of the exodus. Others were performed by men of God. Men of great faith, others were performed by prophets in the Old Testament and there were some prophets in the New Testament as well. And by the apostles, meaning the apostles that Christ chose and Paul, who calls himself an apostle, one who was born out of due season. The book of Acts is filled with the miracles that Paul performed in the cities where he ministered and the people that he touched. It is important to understand that the Bible does not contain a record of all of the miracles that the prophets did, nor does it contain a record of all the miracles the apostles did. It certainly does not contain a record of all the miracles that Jesus did. How do we know that? John 21:25; And there are also many other things which Jesus did, the which, if they should be written, I suppose that even the world itself could not contain the books that should be written. Some theologians say they think that is an embellished statement made by John. John just wrote that there is no way in his opinion, that if you took all the books in the world and filled them with all the miracles that Jesus did on earth, there would not be enough room to hold it all. Remember that John was an eyewitness of these things, so there is a whole lot out there that he either witnessed or heard about that we don't know about. Why did they only deal with specific things? That's a mystery. We don't know why. There are four gospels that are considered to be authentic inspired gospels written by four different writers. Each one wrote from their perspective or how they remembered it.

Luke writes his narrative from the perspective of a medical doctor. What does Luke emphasize? He emphasizes the virgin birth. He goes into detail about Christ being born of a virgin. He goes into detail about the crucifixion. He is the only one that talked about Jesus' sweat becoming as great drops of blood. He is a medical doctor, so he is fascinated by the fact that Jesus is under so much stress that his sweat becomes as great drops of blood. Luke is also the one that talked about life after death. He gives the story of a rich man in hell and a beggar that dies and goes to paradise. No other gospel writer mentions what Luke mentions in Luke chapter sixteen. Why does he talk about this? He talks about it because It is intriguing to him. As a medical doctor, he has to deal with people dying. What happens after death? So, the reason you have different stories is because of the personality of that person who is writing and the interest they have in a particular subject.

Johns' gospel is where most people advice new converts to begin reading their bible at. Johns' gospel is written as an eyewitness who was a personal friend of Jesus. He was so humble, that he wrote his gospel as if he were a third person telling of the events, referring to himself as that disciple whom Jesus loved, instead of bringing attention to himself.

That explains a little bit about the four gospels, now let's get back to the subject of miracles. Miracles produce different results in people. You may say, if God would do a miracle and heal this person, it would shake the town. Think about how people responded to Jesus in his day. The religious Pharisees fought the miracles that Jesus did. They even said it was of the devil. If Jesus raised someone from the dead today, who had been dead for three days, there would be some churches and church people that would say, "I don't believe they were really dead to begin with." They wouldn't even believe the death certificate. They would say it was forged. Look at my own family and people that know us. God brought my daughter Angela, my grandson Lucas, and my husband Dana, all three back from the dead. You would think that would make a powerful impact on people. But most people act like, oh well just another day. Remember the story of Lazarus and the rich man? When the rich man died and found himself in the torments of hell, he asked Jesus to let him return to earth to witness to his five brothers so they would repent and not end up in that place. Jesus told him, they have Moses, and they have the prophets, which is to imply that they have the law of Moses, and all the prophets that have taught the law and showed the way. They have the Torah and the prophets, and if they don't believe that, they are not going to believe one coming back from the dead.

Today we have the written Word, the Bible. We have churches in abundance. The word is preached on TV, radio, Facebook, and You Tube for those who can't get to church and yet there is a battle in our nation over whether or not there is a God.

So, let's think about miracles. The same sun that melts wax, also hardens clay. The same miracle that will take one person and make them say, "WOW there must be a God, will turn another person into a skeptic and they will say, "I don't believe a word of it." "It's all fake." I had some ask me when I was healed of cancer if I had a report to prove it. I heard Tommy Bates giving the testimony of a little girl healed of a brain tumor, and some were trying to say it was a misdiagnosis or mistake somehow. If the glory of God showed up in a service in a cloud, there would be some say, they have a hidden smoke machine in the ceiling. So don't think that miracles will convince everybody that God is real. It didn't in the time of Jesus, and it won't today. However, God's miracles are for the benefit of the person needing it, and they absolutely can convince people in some places in the world that God is real and bring them to salvation.

I was recently reminded of an incident from my teenage years, when me and a cousin of mine was driving our family car up and down the driveway, while my parents were gone. The car died on us about halfway up our driveway and would not start again. After trying repeatedly to start it with no luck, I got a bottle of anointing oil and anointed the hood of the car and prayed asking God to please let the car start so that we could get it back to the house where it belonged. We got back in the car, started it up, drove it to the house and parked it. The reason I was reminded of it was because the cousin that was with me that day had recently gone to church with her brother. She had gotten away from God but when she heard the message she went to an altar and renewed her relationship with Him. After church she told her brother, the story about the car and said, "I remembered how God started the car for Connie that day and it reminded me that God does hear and answer prayer." So, God can perform a miracle today that you may think insignificant and use it years later to touch a heart or minister to a need. And the testimony that comes from it encourages others. I know it did me when my cousin called to tell me about it.

Although not everyone is affected in the same way when witnessing a miracle, it can and does bring many to salvation and into a relationship with God. If we look at the day of Pentecost as it's recorded in Acts 2:16-32 we see many different reactions. It says, they were confounded, they were amazed, they marveled, and some were in doubt. There were some doubters, some were mocking, saying, "look at these men. This isn't God." Out of all these reactions, only one group said, "wow, this is of God" Think about that for a moment. Galileans, speaking in a language they had never spoke before. It's a miracle, but instead of everyone saying, wow, it's the day of Pentecost, this is of God, some are confounded. Some are amazed. Some said, what is this. Some said, I don't believe this, they are just drunk. When God does a great miracle, you are going to get these same reactions today. A lot of it depends on the relationship that the person has with God, as to how they will respond to something God does in the form of a miracle.

Let's look at 7 purposes for a miracle.

1. Mark 16:20; miracles are a sign that the gospel is a true message from God. Signs follow believers to prove the message is truly from God.
2. Matthew 10:7-8; miracles are a sign that the kingdom of heaven is at hand. Jesus said go forth and heal the sick, cleanse the leper, cast out devils, raise the dead and preach that the kingdom of heaven is at hand.
3. John 3:16; It is a sign that God cares for and loves people. For God so loved the world that he gave his son, that none would have to perish. God does miracles because he loves people. God doesn't hate people. God hates sin, but he loves people.
4. Acts 10:38; God performs miracles as a sign to authenticate that the messenger is God's anointed. Not to exalt the messenger but to let the people know that they have been sent from God and that they have this gifting.
5. John 2:23; It's a sign to convince the sinner or unbeliever that God is real. Not all people except that a miracle is real but according to the bible, when one happens, some would believe.
6. Mark 9:6-8; To prove Christ has the power to forgive sins. So that the person who receives a miracle from God can know that the same person who performed that miracle does in reality forgive sins. Forgiveness of sins, healing and miracles go hand in hand.
7. Mark 2:8-12; To bring glory to God and to Christ. Not to exalt the person who prayed, not to exalt the person who receives the miracle. He does it for one reason. That His

name would be great. Remember when Paul comes to the city with one of his companions and the people began to say, the God's are among us. Paul tells them, you must stop this. We are not God's; we are people just like you. Paul does not use that to get a great following, but Paul corrects them immediately, saying this is not about us but about the God of heaven. Let me tell you about Him. God will use people, to see great miracles, if they will always point the attention back to Him and give Him the praise and the glory.

Let's talk about the working of miracles for a moment. In the Greek New Testament, miracles can be alluded to, like a healing or the casting out of devils. The word working of miracles is the word *dunamis*, meaning literally miraculous powers. So, we could say that this is the gift of miraculous powers. Gift of miraculous ability, to see things happen that are impossible for a man to do. Notice it is not just gift of miracles, but it is the gift of working of miracles. That Greek word is where we get the word energy from. It is showing forth something that can be made known, something that can be made visible. So, the idea of a miracle is a supernatural power that enables us to see something visible. Giving us evidence of God's power working on the earth. Notice that miracles are plural not just singular. It's not the working of a miracle, but it's a working of miracles. Because there are different types of miracles.

God still answers prayers, and an answered prayer is a miracle. It's not just answered prayer, but it is miraculous, it is supernatural.

Mark 16:20 reads; And they went forth, and preached everywhere, the Lord working with them, and confirming the word with signs following.

Hebrew 2:4; God also bearing them witness, both with signs and wonders, and with diver's miracles, and the gifts of the Holy Ghost, according to his own will.

These are verses that indicate to us that according to the will of God, miracles still happen. I believe that any biblical miracle we read about, could be repeated in our day and time. As a matter of fact, we have several right here at Victory Tabernacle that can give testimony to the miracles that God has done in this day. I can personally testify of being healed of cancer without any treatments or surgeries. Another sister in the church has been healed of cancer. The greatest testimony I have is when my daughter and grandson were both brought back from the dead. My grandson, whom they said would never be able to talk, and yet he talks even with paralyzed vocal cords. My husband was brought back from the dead and given three more months with us. One of the doctors called him, a modern-day Lazarus, because he was amazed by the miracle. He knew that Dana had been pronounced dead. He knew that they had already ceased to work on him, but here he was. God still works miracles today. He still raises the dead; you just don't hear about it. God has not and will not change.

Healing can be a miracle, but a miracle doesn't always have to be a healing. The multiplication of bread and fish is a miracle but it's not a healing. Putting the ear back on Malcus the servant of the high priest is a miracle but not necessarily healing. It can be classified more as a creative miracle. When praying for healing at times, we should be praying for a miracle. We need to be very specific in our prayer and what we are asking for. We should not be passive but very decisive.

If we need a financial miracle, we need to pray for a provision miracle. We need to ask God to awaken or speak to the spirit of whoever He has that can provide for that need. Sometimes we need to pray for a miracle from the Lord instead of just asking for a word from the Lord or a healing. I heard a story one time about a group of men that had gathered in one of the offices at the stock yard where one of the men worked. They were praying for God to move and meet a financial need for a ministry they were working on. One of the men began to pray specifically, "Lord your word says that you own the cattle on a thousand hills. Would you please sell a few of those cattle and meet this need?" While they were praying, the secretary came into the office and told her boss that there was someone there asking for him and said, "I think you will want to see him." The man stepped out into the outer office and there stood a man who said, "sir, I was just down in the stock yard selling some cattle and God told me to bring you a check for this amount." He handed him a check for the exact amount they were in the office praying and asking God for. God hears and he moves in ways you never thought possible.

Some miracles are on a higher level of manifestation than just that of a healing. Turning water into wine was a miracle. Feeding the multitude with five loaves and two fish was a miracle. That is a little bit of a higher level. In other words, some miracles take a higher level of faith.

Healings are used for a sign and miracles create a wonder. The bible talks about signs and wonders. In the bible healings are often used as a sign that Jesus was the son of God, that he was the Messiah. Miracles were used by Paul as a sign of his apostleship. The signs of an apostle were wrought among you. But what is a bonified miracle? Something that makes people say, "wow", because they know that it took God to do that. If he restores sight instantly to a blind person, you are going to know that it was God. A minister friend of mine, Sister Betty Jones, had x-rays that showed where God put a bone back in her leg that had not been there before. That is a bonified miracle.

Types of miracles found in the scriptures:

There are miracles of healing which include physical and emotional healing. There are miracles of deliverance. Miracles of deliverance include deliverance from demons, demon possession, evil spirits. Also, freedom from depression and oppression, would be considered in the level of a miracle deliverance.

Creative miracles would be multiplication miracles. Miracles of supply. An example of a miracles of supply could be like when Jesus told Peter to go get a fish and he would find a coin in its mouth. He told him to take the coin out of its mouth to pay the taxes. In the

Old Testament an example of a creative miracle could be, when the Israelites wandered in the desert for forty years and their clothes or shoes never wore out.

There are miracles of nature which would include the ability of the Old Testament prophets to produce rain in a drought or suspending nature, like Elijah did, when he said it is not going to rain these years according to my word as a judgment. Another example of suspending nature, found in the New Testament, is Jesus' walking on the water. This was a miracle of nature since ordinarily the law of gravity cannot be broken and yet the law of gravity had to be suspended for both Jesus and Peter to walk on the water. Another instance in the Old Testament (2 Kings 6:6) was where the axe head falls into the water and sinks. The prophet then does something very strange. He cuts a stick and throws it into the water, and it causes an iron axe head to float to the top.

Strange answers to prayer. For example, the prophet Elisha, when he was being mocked by a group of kids, that were making fun of the prophet Elijah that had gone up in the chariot of fire and they are telling Elisha, why don't you go up out of the way? Elisha prayed and bears came out of the woods and ate them. Another strange occurrence or answer to prayer found in the New Testament, (Acts chapter 5) is when Ananias and Sapphira lied about money to Peter and he said, "you have not lied to me but to the Holy Ghost," and for this they were both at two separate times struck dead. There may be other miracles that we could put in other categories but basically most miracles will fall into one of these categories.

Some miracles happen instantaneous or immediately, while others are progressive, and still others are suspended or delayed for a period of time. In Mark chapter five the woman with the issue of blood knew immediately that she had been made whole. She felt it in her body. Some people will know immediately that they have received a miracle. Whether they feel the change within themselves or they can physically see a change.

Sometimes a miracle can be delayed. When Miriam criticized

Moses and received leprosy in Numbers 12:15, Moses cried out for her healing and God said, "no, I won't heal her right now, but I will put her aside for seven days." According to the law, a leper had to go into a camp for seven days, and then be looked at again, to see if the leprosy was still there. God would not break his own law, so he set her aside for those seven days. It could also have been to teach her a lesson. I'm going to show you that you don't talk against the man who has the anointing and is taking care of my business. Sometimes it is a timing issue.

You need to know which gift is needed in each situation. For instance, if someone is in a coma, you don't pray for healing, you pray for a miracle. If an infant is said to be dead in the womb, you don't need to pray for healing, but for a miracle. This happened to my mother with one of my younger brothers. I don't remember how far along she was in her pregnancy but at some point, she was told that they could no longer detect a heartbeat. After giving it some time and checking a couple of more times with no luck, they scheduled her for a surgical procedure to clean out her womb, because they had determined that the baby had died. In the meantime, my mother went to church and had a prayer circle surround her and pray. Pastor Georgia Hughes told her that the surgery would not be necessary because the baby was alive. When mom went in for the procedure, she asked them to check one more time for a heartbeat. Giving all praise and glory to God, the heartbeat had been restored and my little brother was carried to full term she delivered a healthy baby boy.

If a person needs a new organ in their body. For example, their heart needs to be restored. When my husband was ill one of his issues was needing another heart by-pass that they were unable to do. After prayer and another test, they found that new veins or arteries had grown around his heart, which effectively by-passed the blockage. They said they didn't know how but the heart had apparently repaired itself. But I say to God be the glory! He knows our need and what needs to be done to fix it.

Another testimony that I heard and love to share is one given by Pastor Bates. He said that there was an individual in his church that needed a liver transplant. After having test run, she went in for a consultation and was told that her liver no longer needed to be replaced. She thought the doctor was holding something back, so she pressed him wanting to know what else he had found or wasn't telling her. The doctor said there is no explanation for it but there was a picture of a perfect fingerprint on her liver in the scan. Isn't God awesome?

Why do miracles sometimes not happen? Let's look at four times in the scriptures that miracles failed and ask ourselves why and find out what happened.

1. In Numbers chapter 12, When Moses asked God to heal Miriam from leprosy and God said no. It was not a permanent no but a temporary no, and seven days later she was healed. So sometimes if you feel like it is not happening, it can be a timing issue. Maybe there is a more appropriate time or better time for this to happen.

2. In 2 Kings chapter 4; When Gehazi prayed for the dead boy to be raised, it didn't happen. Why couldn't Gehazi lay the rod on the boy's body the way the prophet told him to, and the boy be healed? It was because Gehazi's heart was not right with God. God was not going to use him, and let him walk around and say, "did you see what I did?" God knew he had pride in his heart.

3. In Mark 8:22; When Jesus prayed for the blind man to be healed, he did not get an instant healing at that moment, but only a partial healing. Jesus did not fail in the miracle he only had to pray again. This is a great example of praying more than once when someone needs a miracle. There could be a couple of reasons why this happened. One reason could be that they were in Bethsaida and this was a city that Jesus had cursed because of their unbelief, so Jesus took the man

outside the city to pray for him. Another reason could be that Jesus was setting an example for us to ask and keep asking. Seek and keep seeking. Knock and keep knocking until we have peace that God has heard us.

4. Matthew 17, when the disciples prayed for the epileptic boy nine disciples failed in praying to cast the spirit out of the boy. Because of a lack of faith in the disciples. When the disciples asked, "why could we not do this?" Jesus answered and said, "because of your unbelief." He also said that this kind comes about by fasting and prayer.

In the process of gaining a miracle faith is required. Faith can be a gift, but it can also be a fruit. In Luke 5:20 Jesus saw their faith. In Acts 14:9, Paul perceived that the man had faith to be healed.

A special anointing is often required for there to be a miracle. There are levels of the anointing. Sometimes the level of anointing is determined by the atmosphere or by the faith of the people. Sometimes there needs to be an act of faith, or a demonstration. A point of contact. Something that helps to release your faith. Examples are prayer clothes and anointing oil. We have also prayed over soap, corn meal, salt, and things like that to help people to believe and release their faith, so that God can move in their situation. If any two or three agree, touching any one thing it shall be done. You can agree together and pray over an object, and it can go forth and bring conviction, deliverance, healing, whatever the need is that you are praying for. Special miracles often use a thing or an object. (Examples: David's sling, Moses' rod, Paul's handkerchiefs and aprons, Peters shadow). A special miracle wrought by God often uses a tool of faith. Something that connects with that person.

GIFT OF HEALING

NOW WE ARE GOING TO LOOK INTO THE GIFTS OF HEALING WHICH is the fourth gift listed in 1 Corinthians chapter twelve and verse nine.

As we begin let's take a look at Exodus 15:26; And said, if thou wilt diligently hearken to the voice of the Lord thy God, and wilt give ear to his commandments, and keep all his statutes, I will put none of these diseases upon thee, which I have brought upon the Egyptians: for I am the Lord that healeth thee. This is called the healing covenant verse given to the nation of Israel. Notice that God gave stipulations of what they had to do in order to receive the benefit of the healing. That was total obedience to the Word and to God. Many times, we have a give me attitude and fail to recognize that we have a part or something that we have to do to obtain the promises of God.

The second thing is that God not only established a covenant with Israel, but God established a covenant name that identifies Him as a healer. In the Old Testament we have what is called compound names. That is where two names are put together. There are compound names for God. The name that God gave for Himself to Moses is spelled in four Hebrew letters (YHWH), we pronounce it Yahweh. Yahweh is the sacred name of God. When you add a word, such as God the healer, it becomes a compound word, Jehovah-Rapha. Jehovah-Shalom is God our peace. Jehovah-Nissi is God our banner. There are at least sixteen of these major names found in the Old Testament. Using the term Yahweh begins in Exodus and goes all the way through to the book of Malachi. In Exodus 15:26 there is a reference to Isaiah 53:5, which says by His stripes we are healed. But the name that is found in Exodus 15:26, I am the Lord that healeth thee, is Yahweh-Rapha. If you take the Hebrew word *Rafpha,* and you look at the meaning of it, there are some very interesting things about the word. The meaning of the word Rapha in the Hebrew is to restore to a previously enjoyed state. Or a previously enjoyed condition meaning, I was healthy, now I am sick, but God is going to restore me back to health. Also, it means to mend by stitching. Where does the idea come from to mend by stitching? In the ancient days stitching refers to a weaving machine. The weaving machines back then had rocks to hold them down, and when the weaving machine would begin to be run by hand those rocks would beat together and make a sound. Now throughout scripture God is described as our rock, so when the rocks would bang together and make that sound and weaving began to take place, it gave the illusion or the idea, that God is the one that weaves you back together or of God stitching you back together. This may be why the writer says he heals the broken of heart and binds up their wounds. So Jehova-Rapha is the one that restores you back to a previously enjoyed state or condition.

Third we know that healing was promised by the prophets. In Isaiah 53:5 it says, "But he was wounded for our transgressions, he was bruised for our iniquities: the chastisement of our peace was upon him; and with his stripes we are healed."

Now pay attention in this verse to the word stripes. Because the Hebrew word used here for stripes is a word that means black or blue wounds. It refers to a bruise of some kind that can be visibly seen on the body. We remember that before Jesus went to the cross, he was taken to the whipping post where he was scourged. The scourging was done with whips that had metal and glass embedded in them so that not only would he be bruised but he would also have open wounds where the glass and metal dug in and tore the flesh. So, we have Isaiah prophesying that by his wounds you are healed, and then if we look in the New Testament (1 Peter 2:24) Peter says, "by his stripes you were healed." So, Isaiah the prophet is looking forward to a time when Jesus stripes would bring healing and Peter the apostle is looking back to the time when the prophesy was fulfilled through the stripes of Jesus Christ. Healing was promised by the prophets of the Old Testament such as Isaiah, that the Messiah would bring healing.

A fourth example of a prophetic scripture with healing can be found in Malachi 4:2 which says, "But unto you that fear my name shall the son of righteousness arise with healing in his wings, and ye shall go forth, and grow up as calves of the stall." What is the idea of wings? Birds have wings, some angels have wings (seraphim's, found in Zechariah) but people don't have wings.

The word wings in Hebrew is *kanaph* (kaw-nawf), and it means a border, a corner and it also means the skirt. In the law of Moses, it was commanded that the men would wear what is called *tzitzit's*, which are strings attached to their garments that represented certain aspects of God's word and law. Later in history, something developed called a *tallit*. *Tallits* have been used for a long time, and they were used in the times of Jesus.

The phylacteries and the Tallit's are what we call prayer shawls today. When you drape a prayer shawl around yourself, there are four corners. Those four corners have threads that are called Tzitzits. There are references to this that says there must be a blue thread woven into those. Blue is heavenly. The blue thread on a tallit represents the healing covenant. Jesus being Jewish and being in the synagogue at times, would have had tzitzits on him, maybe even a prayer shawl, but definitely at the bottom of his garment. In Mark chapter 5 we have the story of the woman with the issue of blood. And she said, "if I can just touch the hem of is garment, I shall be made whole." Anybody being Rabbinical or Jewish would have understood what she was doing. The tzitzit, the strings that hang down from a Jewish man's garment which were on the hem of Jesus garment, represent healing. Scripture tells us that many of them sought to touch the hem of his garment. This is a reference to a healing that the Messiah brings. It is the Messiah that would introduce healing through his garment in the time that he would arrive.

It is important to understand that when you are ministering to people that need healing that they understand that God has promised long life. You have to encourage them and claim the promise of long life found in Exodus 20:12; Honor thy father and thy mother: that thy days may be long upon the earth. Psalm 91:16; with long life will I satisfy him and show him my salvation. Proverbs 3:2; For length of days, and long life, and peace, shall be added to thee. There are numerous verses in the bible that indicate that obedience to God, obeying your father and mother are going to bring or add a long life. We need to encourage people to believe God that they can have a long life, as it relates to the possibility of God healing them when sickness or disease comes into their body.

Notice in the text that Paul wrote that this is not a gift of healing, but it is gifts of healing. Gifts is plural and the implication is that there are various ways which a person can be healed. Let's take a look at some of the various ways in the bible that God wrought healing.

1. Healing can be wrought by an angel of the Lord. In John chapter 5, it says that at the pool of Bethesda by the sheep market there was a certain season, that an angel of the Lord would come and trouble the water, and that the first person to enter in the water would be healed. The angel is not named but obviously it happened, because the man said, someone always gets in before me. So, it is obvious that all these sick people are there and that there have seen people healed. They know something is happening and that it involves an angel. An interesting side note is that church tradition tells us who that angel was. Church tradition tells

us that there are seven arch angels. Two of them in our bible are Michael and Gabriel. One of the angels was noted in one of the Apocrypha books which was in the 1611 King James Version. The book of Tobit in the Apocrypha tells us about an angel by the name of Raphael. Raphael is an angel that allegedly brought healing to the people at the pool of Bethesda. If you listen to the name Raphael, what name do you hear in it? Raffah which means heal and El which in Hebrew is another name for God. So, the name Raphael means God heals. So because the name means that and because of the book of Tobit and because of church tradition, there was a tradition that God has a healing angel, and that angels name is Rafael. Can this be proven? No, it can't. But it is proven according to John chapter 5 that angels can bring healing.

2. Another form of healing is by speaking the word. Psalm107:20, He sent forth his word, and healed them. Matthew 8:8, The centurion answered and said, Lord, I am not worthy that thou shouldest come under my roof: but speak the word only, and my servant shall be healed. I like to share personal testimonies, when possible, to help us see that God has not changed. When my youngest son, David, was around two or three years old, he began running a fever. There was church that night and I was going to take him to be prayed for. My husband wanted to keep him home with him, so I went without him. When the spirit was moving, I went to the pastor and told him that I had a sick baby at home and needed prayer for him. We agreed in prayer and the pastor told me to check the time and when I got home to ask my husband what time our son's fever broke. When I got home, I asked how David was doing. My husband said that suddenly, the fever had left, and he had been up playing. I asked what time the fever left, and it was at the exact time that the pastor and I had agreed in prayer and spoke to the

fever and sickness. God does not change. So, in other word, the power of speaking the word, both the word of God and speaking over a person. Quoting scriptures to them can actually bring healing.

3. Healing can come though the laying on of hands. Luke 4:40, Now when the sun was setting, all they that had any sick with divers' diseases brought them unto him; and he laid his hands on every one of them and healed them. Some people who are not familiar with church might ask, why do you lay hands on people? It is a doctrine of the church that began with the early church. Hebrews 6:2 says, Of the doctrine of baptisms, and of laying on of hands, and of resurrection of the dead, and of eternal judgment. This scripture shows us that laying on of hands was a doctrine of the early church. They would lay hands upon those that were being ordained into the ministry. Paul said he laid hands on Timothy to impart spiritual gifts. In Acts 19:6, they laid hands on people to receive the baptism of the Holy Ghost. In the New Testament, it is most commonly used in praying for the sick. In the ministry of Jesus especially, he commissioned them, and they lay hands on the sick. In the book of James, it says to lay hands on the sick and they shall recover. So, the laying on of hands is very significant.

However, if a person is praying for someone without an anointing and the person being prayed for doesn't have faith, it is the equivalent of laying empty hands on empty heads. Because you will discover that nobody receives anything. It's not that God doesn't hear the prayer but there must be an anointing, and there has to be faith. That's why so many times you will hear a preacher say, get in while the water is troubled. That is why you will notice that the gifts come into operation either during worship or while a preacher is preaching. That is when the anointing is strongest. That is the best time to seek healing.

I would like to say at this time, that it is also possible to lay hands on other things and have God move. When David was a baby, I was washing a load of diaper when my washer stopped working. I didn't have my babies in the pampers era, so we used cloth diapers and I had filled the washer and it had started the wash cycle when all of a sudden it shut down. I pushed buttons, turned knobs, did everything that I could think of to do. Then I began to pray. I told the Lord how badly I needed those diapers washed, like he didn't already know. Then I said Lord, you said you would supply all of my need, and this is what I need right now. I felt the anointing rise up as I prayed, so I got the anointing oil, and I laid my hands on the washing machine and prayed. I turned the machine back on and it started up and didn't die again for several years. God is good in all things. I have a lot more testimonies like that, but I will try to keep them to a minimum.

The laying on of hands is quite simply, the power of God in you being released out from you to the person or object that you are praying for.

4. Healing through faith. Maybe someone will come to you, and you may not feel it, but they say, "I believe if you lay hands on me and pray, I will be healed." If you are under the anointing, you can lay hands on them and pray, and your anointing can be released into their faith level and healing can take place. Look at the woman in the bible (Mark 5:25) with the issue of blood. Jesus is in a crowd, and the woman makes her way to him. She touches the hem of his garment, and he stops and says, "Who touched me?" The disciples asked, "What do you mean, who touched you?" There are so many people moving around, how do you know somebody touched you? And Jesus responds with, "because I felt virtue go out of me." The word virtue is translated here from the same Greek word used in the book of Acts that said you

shall receive power. The word power and the word virtue both come from the Greek word, *dunamis.* It is a miraculous ability through the power of God, or the miraculous power of God. So, when she touched him, she pulled something out of him that he felt leave him. He didn't see her, he didn't know she was back there, as the disciples pointed out, it was a large crowd. But her faith was so strong that when she touched him, the power went out of him into her body and instantly she was healed. Preachers who are used in the gift of healing when they have prayed for multiple people, will become weak in their own body from the drain of the anointing that is being pulled from them.

If you will take notice, when you are in a church setting, and God begins to move whether it be a healing or miracle or whatever gift comes into action, it releases people's faith in the crowd. They begin to get excited. It stirs their faith. Now some people have their faith in a certain preacher, or they think if we just have a revival, it will happen in the revival meeting. Your faith must be in God. It is never to be about the person that he uses. We are his vessels the tools that he uses to perform his word. He will use whoever he chooses, wherever he chooses, whenever he chooses, if you will only believe. The same God that shows up in revival, is already in the house during every service, it is just a matter of where is your faith? When your faith level rises, God shows up in your circumstance. So, when you quit seeking a revival and start seeking the reviver. When you quit waiting for your favorite preacher to come and get in touch with the ultimate preacher. When you quit looking for what you think things should be and open your heart and mind to receive whatever God brings, in whatever form he brings it, you will begin to live in a revival atmosphere. When we understand that it's not about the song or who sings it. It's not about who brings the message, but it's about the God who ordained it. When the living Word shows up, when the anointing shows up, when glory shows up that's when heaven comes down and you just have to wait your turn. Have you ever had someone lay hands on you and you felt like electricity was going through your body? That is the anointing. I've had people tell me that they felt a warmth go through them. It is the anointing.

5. Healing with the use of anointing oil. James 5:14-15 says, Is any sick among you? Let him call for the elders of the church; and let them pray over him anointing him with oil in the name of the Lord: 15. And the prayer of faith shall save the sick, and the Lord shall raise him up; and if he has committed any sins, they shall be forgiven him. When scripture says him, it also applies to her, so him or her will be forgiven. Here we are looking at a church setting. If there be any among you sick let him call for the elders of the church. When you come to God for healing, he also forgives you of any sin in your life before he heals you. Look at the ministry of Jesus. When he prayed for people what did he say first? He said thy sins be forgiven thee, then arise and walk or be ye healed, whatever the circumstance might be. So, in the healing process, the forgiveness of sins is connected with the miracle of healing. Because salvation and healing go together. We will be discussing this later when we come to the atonement. But salvation should never be made hard. Salvation is believing upon the Lord. People complicate being saved. Jesus said, whosoever believes on me shall be saved. Look at the thief on the cross. He simply said, Lord remember me when you come into your kingdom. And Jesus replied, this day will you be with me in paradise. This does not mean that you don't have to repent. In Matthew 3:2, it says, Repent ye: for the kingdom of heaven is at hand. Luke 13:5 say's, except you repent, you shall perish. I'm saying you have to believe before you can repent or before you

can receive from God. Act 2:21 and Romans 10:3 both say whoever calls on the name of the Lord shall be saved. The belief is as important as the confession. God is looking at the heart and the approach of that person in their faith. If you can't believe that he has the power to forgive your sins, then neither can you believe that he can heal you, deliver you, or whatever your need that you are petitioning for. According to the book of James when he heals, he also forgives. Now going back to James 5:14-15. According to this scripture it is important that they anoint with oil, but the oil does not do the healing. Why do we anoint with oil? The oil represents the Holy Spirit. In the Old Testament, when the oil came upon David, the Spirit came upon David. Psalms 133:1-2; Behold how good and pleasant [it is] for brethren to dwell together in unity! 2. [It is] like the precious ointment upon the head that ran down upon the beard, [even] Aaron's beard: that went down to the skirts of his garments; Since the oil represents the Spirit and in the Old Testament under the old covenant, when the oil was poured upon someone the Spirit would come upon them, then the early church began to associate the idea that oil and the Holy Spirit work together, so if we anoint them with oil it draws the Holy Spirit. So, the bottom line as to why we use oil, is obedience to the word of God. No other reason. Just that God said to do it, James was inspired to write it, so that is why we do it.

6. Healing by rebuking spirits. Matthew 17:18, And Jesus rebuked the devil; and he departed out of him: and the child was cured from that very hour. Mark 1:25; And Jesus rebuked him, saying, hold thy peace, and come out of him. Please remember that not everything in a sickness is demonic. It takes the discerning of Spirits to determine if a spirit is involved or not involved. But when a spirit is involved, the spirit must be rebuked in the name of the Lord Jesus Christ.

7. Healing through the Lord's Supper. Acts 2:46; and breaking bread from house to house every day. If you look at some of the older commentaries, you will see that it says they were going house to house and conducting the Lord's Supper every single day. Perry Stone wrote a book titled, "The Meal That Heals," based on Dr. John Miller who had a revelation on healing through the Lord's Supper. And they proved from the bible, from scripture and from history, that there were so many being saved in the early church that they wanted to introduce to them, the Lord's Supper and what it means. The Lord Jesus took the bread and said this represents my body (which was broken for our healing) and this cup represents my blood (which was shed for our salvation), do this in remembrance of me. It reminds us that he and he alone has paid the price for our healing and our salvation. It represents the new covenant and when you take it, you are joining in covenant with him. Another thing that it says in the bible, is that you should search yourself, or judge yourself before you take it, that you don't bring condemnation upon yourself. By judging yourself, you get all the stuff out of you like, unforgiveness, envy, strife, whatever shouldn't be there. When it comes to scripture you learn that when you partake of the Lord's Supper you must be worthy of it. So, you should always search your heart to get all of that stuff out of you before you participate in the Lord's Supper. Many people who seek healing are not healed because of unforgiveness. Because of strife. Because they are harboring some kind of sin. Please know that this is not all cases, but there are so many people in the church that are holding on to bitterness, strife, and unforgiveness and you are trying to pray over top of this and they are not confessing it out. That is why the warning is given with the Lord's Supper not to take it unworthily because, Paul said, for this reason many are weak, many are sickly, and many

sleep because they do not discern the body of Christ. So first repent. Maybe something slipped in while you weren't watching. Root it out, ask God to take out of you everything that shouldn't be there and if any sin, maybe it's a sin I am not aware of, Lord cleanse me right now in the name of the Lord, and what it does, it gets all of that stuff out of your spirit making it easier for the Holy Spirit to move on you, to bless you and bring healing to your body.

What receiving healing requires. Healing often requires an act of faith. In 2 Kings 5:10, A prophet told a general to go dip in the Jordan river seven times. The problem was not dipping seven times, the problem was in Naaman's response, which was that the Jordan was muddy and the rivers at home had clean water. He said, "I could have just stayed in my own country and done this." The answer is no. He couldn't have stayed home in his own country and been healed. He had to have an act of faith. In John 5:8, Jesus tells a man, take up your bed and walk. The man must make an effort to act out his faith. A lot of time God may require someone to act out their faith because healing often requires God seeing someone's actions in order for them to be healed. James 2:26 talks about faith without works is dead. Another way of saying it is that faith without action corresponding to it is dead. In other words, sometimes God wants you to do something or take some kind of action. He sees the action such as when the men tore the roof up to get their friend in to Jesus. The scripture said, he saw their faith. Have you ever heard the saying; action speaks louder than words? It's an old saying but it is very true.

To be used in the gift of healing you have to feel compassion for people. If you see someone that is ill or has a physical handicap and you say poor guy, God bless him, but you are not moved with compassion you will probably not be used in the gift of healing. Compassion is one of the big triggers that stirs you to want people to be healed. There needs to have been preaching of the word that brings out the healings and works of Jesus in the bible. That is how our faith to receive what God has for us takes root and grows. My mom used to tell me that a person needs to be sitting under a ministry where their faith can be built before God can move in their situation. Remember a big part of God moving in us is that we have to believe. We have to have faith. The word tells us that faith cometh by hearing and hearing by the word of God.

Also, to be used in the gift you need to have an anointing because it is the anointing that destroys the yoke. It also helps if you have discernment, so that you know if you are dealing with a spirit or not.

We need to note also that healing is part of what is known as the atonement. It doesn't take the gifts of healing for someone to be healed, it simply takes the prayer of faith for someone to be healed. Meaning that if no one in the congregation has the gifts of healing, we can still pray for the sick. We know this because James said, if you are sick, call for the elders of the church to anoint them and pray over them and the prayer of faith will save the sick and the Lord God will raise them up. So, he knew there may not always be someone with the gifts of healing in the congregation, my thought is for instance, some of the churches that don't go as deep into the word may not have the gifts but can still pray for the sick and see God move for them. Even in our full gospel churches, how many people do you know besides Peter that had such a strong anointing that they can heal someone with their shadow. How many people do you know like Paul that could lay hands on a handkerchief and demons would come out of people? These are special miracles. Not everyone is going to operate in that way. God made a provision for people to be healed because he placed it in the atonement.

The word atonement, the old English word, means at-one-ment. What it actually refers to is that God reconciles himself back to man and man back to him. Now a nominal church mostly has one emphasis on the atonement and that would be salvation. In a Pentecostal or full gospel church we emphasize both salvation and healing. However, if you go back and read Isaiah chapter 53 you will see that you are not just a body or a soul, but you are also a spirit. So, the atonement must be three-fold. It has to affect the body; it has to bring reconciliation to the physical body. It has to bring reconciliation to the human spirit. Some kind of reconciliation to the mind if it is going to be a real atonement. So, Christ performed an atonement of bringing men back to God, in body, soul, and spirit.

How do we know that? First of all, 1 Thessalonians tells us, And the very God of peace sanctify you wholly; and I pray God your whole spirit and soul and body be preserved blameless unto the Lord Jesus Christ. If you read Isaiah 53 in its entirety, it is the best messianic prophecy of Jesus in the entire bible. It reveals a threefold atonement. Jesus' soul was made a sin offering. In other words, he died on behalf of transgression. He took our transgressions upon himself, his soul becoming a sin offering, which was the atonement for our eternal life. That's the spirit. He redeemed my spirit because my spirit is eternal. We receive this atonement when we accept him as our Savior.

Isaiah 53:5 says, by his stripes we are healed, and Peter says by his stripes you were healed. He took the stripes for physical disease. Matthew 8:17 says, Himself took our infirmities, and bare our sicknesses. So, he took an atonement for our physical healing. Now here is the one that gets left out. The soulish realm. The soul. Body, soul, and spirit. He carried our grief's, he carried our sorrows, the chastisement of our peace was upon him. He was oppressed on our behalf. What does that mean? Oppression, grief, and sorrow are all emotions. They can affect the body, they can affect the spirit, but it all begins in the mind or the soulish realm. So, in the atoning work of Jesus, we should emphasize that not only can God heal your spirit, where you are separated from God, and take care of your sin making you whole on the inside. God can heal your physical body. We know that from the ministry of Jesus in the New Testament, that's all promised. We need to also let people know that God can heal all of the emotional stuff that they deal with. There are people who have been through divorce that are still completely wounded. There are people that have lost loved ones through accidents and death, and they are still trying to figure out, God why? There are people that live under oppression. Some people call it manic depression, some people call it by-polar, there are all kinds of medical terms people give to things that probably have a spiritual root to it. Not always but a lot of times. We need to be teaching healing is for the whole man. God wants us to be whole. To be whole is to be complete. For example, if you are in great physical shape and you love the Lord with all of your heart, but you are an emotional wreck all the time and your mind is tormented. Then you are not whole. If we say we are full gospel, meaning that we believe it all, then we also need to be full atonement. Jesus doesn't just save you. Let's go to the next level, Jesus can heal you physically. Let's go to the next level, Jesus can heal you emotionally. Where you're not tormented at night, where you're not oppressed and where you're not down all the time. He can change all of that. I felt like this was important for us to look at and recognize today because in the last few years, I have dealt with so many people that are being attacked in their minds. I think it is important that we recognize that God can heal our mind as well as our body and spirit. There is nothing impossible with God and he is concerned about your whole being. Jesus said to the man at the pool of Bethesda in John 5:6, wilt thou be made whole. In Matthew 15:28, And her daughter was made whole. Jesus wants us to be whole. To be complete. He wants an army that is spiritually stable, physically able, and mentally alert.

This is a message that people need to hear, but at the same time, there must be people raised up that seek God. We need to pray and ask God for the gift because you can't receive if you don't ask. Also, Paul said to stir up that gift that is within you. Don't be satisfied to just say I have it but press into God where you can be used effectively in it.

THE GIFT OF FAITH

WHAT IS THE DIFFERENCE IN FAITH AND THE GIFT OF FAITH? Romans 12:3 tells us that every man is given a measure of faith. We must have faith to believe in God. We must have faith to obtain salvation. Matthew 17:20 tells us that if we have faith the size of a grain of mustard seed we can speak to the mountain and say be thou removed, and it will be moved. Luke 17:6 gives a similar view when the Lord said, if you had faith as a grain of mustard seed, you could say to the sycamine tree, be thou plucked up by the root, and be thou planted in the sea, and it should obey you. Now I think that is some big action for such a small amount of faith. But there are times when you need a faith that surpasses your regular faith. You need the faith of the Holy Ghost to power you up, which is the gift of faith. The gift of faith is the supernatural ability to believe for the impossible without doubting or wavering. The gift of faith is not about moving God but to give you a level of faith to believe that your prayer is being heard and answered. It is to help you in your confidence level. The gift of faith is necessary to you more than ordinary faith when it's needed to bring a manifestation of healing or miracles from God. Praying for example for a person near death in an accident, or a person dying in a hospital may require a special level of faith to trigger confidence in the person praying. The bible says if our heart condemns us, we don't have confidence toward God. So, we must get condemnation out of our heart. He said we have to ask in faith believing with nothing wavering. When you pray you are praying in faith? Meaning you may not be feeling anything supernatural, but you are asking in faith expecting to receive. But when there is great need, where God is going to perform a miracle, then the supernatural power of faith rises up and you speak with a greater authority and boldness.

I have a personal testimony that I believe will help demonstrate the difference between regular everyday faith and the gift of faith. My daughter was in her seventh month of pregnancy with her second child when she began to have problems. We had taken her to the hospital to be checked out and the doctor thought she was having gall bladder problems and sent her back home. About four o'clock in the morning, I was woken up, hearing a voice saying, "pray for your babies." I immediately got up and began to pray. A little later that day we had to take her back to the hospital. This time she was rushed from the local hospital to the UK Medical Center in Lexington. I followed behind the ambulance, and I could see the medical team working on her on the drive up there. I kept praying because I knew something was not right. Not long after arrival, I saw her eyes glaze over. The doctor and nurses went into action and immediately rushed her out of the room to surgery. Someone came back to me and told me that they were trying to stabilize her and that they were going to try to save the baby. I asked when I would be able to see her. I was then told that they had lost her and were working on her, trying to get her back and stabilize her. I felt a change take place within me. Fear and worry were pushed aside, and I began to pray with a power and a purpose that I hadn't felt before. I spoke life and healing into both my daughter and my grandson. I reminded God that I had been woken up at four o'clock that morning to pray for my babies and I had obeyed that command. There was absolutely no doubt in my mind that God was going to do what I was asking. I didn't believe the report that was being given to me, I believed God. There is so much more to this story but the point that I want to make is that at a time when my normal faith was not strong enough to pray and believe the way that I needed to, the gift of faith took over and I was able to speak with an authority that I didn't know I had. We later found out that Angela's sugar had gone so high that it had caused her placenta to rupture, and it had burst. We were also told later, and it is recorded in the medical records, that my daughter died on the table and my grandson was born dead. But thanks to an awesome God who has not changed, that's not the end of the story. He still raises the dead. He still places the gifts within us and pulls them up as they are needed. At this time my grandson is twenty-one years old and going strong. We were told that he would have learning disabilities because of the lack of oxygen to his brain for too long of a period of time. Three years ago, I was honored to attend his high school graduation, along with his mother who is alive and well and preaching the gospel. I give God all praise and glory. I am thankful for Holy Ghost power and the gifts that God has given to his church!

So, the gift of faith needs to be imparted especially when there is a dangerous life-threatening situation you are dealing with, such as death or a disease that can take a person's life. That is when you to need the gift of faith to be in operation.

Hebrews 11:1 says, now faith is the substance of things hoped for. The Greek word for substance means to stand up under. Faith is the thing that causes us to stand up under the pressure and the weight to keep hoping that something is going to happen. And the evidence of things not yet seen. That word evidence in the Greek means conviction, the firm conviction of knowing. Knowing that you have not yet seen it but it's going to happen. In Hebrews 11:6, it says that it is impossible to please God without faith.

Hebrews 11 is often called the faith chapter of the bible and it mentions fourteen people in the Old Testament of the bible that by faith did tremendous feats. It's important to understand that faith is what comes into our heart that helps us to be able to stand with a firm conviction that what we are believing for is absolutely going to happen.

Now there are some faith facts that I would like to share with you. The word faith is mentioned two hundred and forty-seven times in the English translation of the King James bible. It is mentioned two hundred and forty-five times in the New Testament but only two times in the Old Testament. Now, here is a question. Why would faith be mentioned in the Old Testament only two times in thirty-nine books, and yet in only twenty-seven books in the New Testament it is mentioned two hundred and forty-five times? First of all, in the two places where it is mentioned in the Old Testament it is the Hebrew word *Emunah* (a-moon) and you can almost hear amen in that. It is a word that means to be firm or secure. The just shall live by faith. When you say *Emunah* (a-moon) in the Hebrew and translate it to English, it means, so be it and it is firm. It means to be firm or secure. The just shall live by faith. The just shall be secure in trusting God. That's an Old Testament verse. But in the New Testament, the Greek word for faith is *Pistis* (peace-tus) which means persuasion, or trusting what God said. So, the question was, why was it found only twice in the Old Testament and two hundred forty-five times in the New Testament? I believe the answer is this. The Old Testament is based on obeying laws. The New Testament is based on faith in the redemptive work of Christ. In other words, in the Old Testament, you did this, and you didn't do this because you had to meet the requirements of the law. The old covenant is based on promises, and those promises are activated by faith. According to the word (Hebrews 6:12 and Hebrews 11:33) by faith and patience we inherit the promises that God gives us in the word.

Faith is a gift that is activated in the heart the moment we begin to accept the bible and we begin to believe what it says. Romans 10:10 says, with the heart man believeth unto righteousness, and with the mouth confession is made unto salvation. Faith is defined as God's divine persuasion, or to be persuaded to fully trust God and to trust his word. If a person is not persuaded, they don't have faith. But if a person is persuaded that is a sign that faith is in their heart. Now the Greek word *pistis* (peace-tus) is a word that refers to, like in the gift of faith, God enabling a person to believe his word and take him at his word. In Greek mythology, this particular Greek word we find in the New Testament for faith, referred to the personification of God, the reliability and trust. In the ancient time the word *pistis* (peace-tus) referred to the guarantee of something like a warranty. The idea was to give evidence of or proof of a statement. So, faith is the evidence, for us, of things not yet seen based on the statement that God has given us in his word. The two hundred and forty-five times that this word for faith is used in the New Testament, it is used to give evidence or proof of a statement. This is some interesting history about the Greek word for faith. The Greek's thought that *pistis* (peace-tus) was the subject that could introduce a particular state of mind to the listener. The subject then appeals to the intellect and rational aspect of the mind. Then the use of logical and rational thinking concerning the issue or thought being discussed are all connected around this word.

Basically, we have the word of God which is our facts our truth. So, faith is the ability to be able to wholly completely take the thoughts of God and as we absorb and think on the thoughts of God, we believe what it says. We claim a promise that we don't see happen because faith is a substance of things hoped for and evidence or confidence of things not yet seen. One of the most fascinating studies of all the gifts actually is the gift of faith, because it is amazing when you see people that have never heard the gospel preached before under the anointing (for example a foreign mission field or someone that has not been in church or maybe they have been in a church where the anointing is not present) and for the first time they start believing what they hear, because there is a power behind the preaching of the word of God. Because they feel something. They did not know the presence of God could be felt. When they feel the presence of God for the first time, and they are hit with the power of the Holy Spirit it causes faith to grow and suddenly rise up inside them. God imparts on you the power of the ability of believing.

Biblical faith is from the heart, the mind, and also from the spirit. You believe with the heart, you reason with the mind, but the power is felt in your spirit. Your believing begins in the heart, because they have now proven that the heart has a brain of its own, so the heart has feeling and emotion. So, with the heart you believe and with the mind you reason and you are able to think and process information, but the power that seals what's in the heart and in the brain through the anointing comes by faith which is where the miraculous begins to happen.

There is a word in Romans10:17, faith cometh by hearing, and hearing by the word of God. The Greek word for word used in this verse is *Rhema* (ray-ma). *Rhema* is a specific word given at a specific time for a specific situation. Now think about this. If faith comes by hearing the word preached, why doesn't everybody in the church have faith? If word comes by hearing the pastor's sermon preached and it should build everybody's faith, why does half the people leave excited and half are saying I don't know about that message, it didn't do anything for me? How can you preach a message and half of them say that was powerful, I got something out of it, I was encouraged, and the other half say well it didn't do a thing for me? If faith comes by hearing something must happen in your ears first. Jesus said, he that hath ears, let him hear what the spirit saith to the churches. The word has to enter through the ears, enter the mind and be dropped into your spirit. It comes by hearing the *Rhema* not *logos*. The *logos* of God is the doctrine, the teaching, the sayings, and the bible. The *logos* of God is the word made flesh. Christ is the word made flesh; the *logos* made flesh. But when the bible talks about in Ephesians, faith cometh by the word of God, that's *Rhema*. Take the sword of the Spirit, which is the word of God, that's *Rhema*. And *Rhema* according to Vine's dictionary is not the whole bible but it is a specific word from the bible for a specific situation or for a specific time.

Now this is how faith comes. Have you ever heard somebody preach something and all of a sudden, they quoted a verse or gave a word study and it quickened you? Suddenly it hits you and you say, oh, that's it. Suddenly, your spirit starts turning. That's the answer to that problem, that's what I need to do. What just happened is faith hit you because the word became alive. A *Rhema* word must be quickened into your spirit. It has to be made alive into your spirit. That's why people who enter a church that does not believe in the manifestation of the Holy Spirit and does not believe in the baptism of the Holy Spirit, if you follow how they are with their faith, they have a very low level of faith. You tell them that God heals or that he still does miracles, and they say, I don't know about that. I don't believe that. The only level of faith that they have is the salvation level. They preach salvation. They can get people saved but beyond that there is nothing. Just the basics. And salvation will get you to heaven, praise God for that, it is the greatest gift in the world. But my point is to have faith in the miraculous, to get answers to prayer, to have healing and miracles, there has to be a level of believing connected to that. Not unbelief but belief in order for those miracles and for the operation or the manifestation for those gifts to begin to take place. So *Rhema* is the word that God brings faith out of because he makes that particular word come alive in your spirit.

The gift of faith usually operates after the preaching of the word because God uses the word first. You can read this in the ministry of Jesus. He sat and taught them first and then prayed for the sick. Most of the time you will notice that Jesus was teaching when people would come and then he performed miracles. Whether he was in someone's home, or the synagogue, wherever he was, usually teaching came first. An example is when they lowered a man through the roof as he was teaching, and he healed him. In the bible Paul said he perceived in his heart that the man had faith to be healed while he was teaching. Most of the time faith comes into people's heart while there is teaching or preaching of the word because this is the principle of what God said. So once again *Rhema* is a word that is spoken at a specific time for a specific situation. Once you get a *Rhema* word from God you can't get away from it. There is a confidence level that gets into your spirit, and you know that you know. When you have heard from God yourself then nothing or nobody can convince you otherwise.

When I first started Victory Tabernacle, I had people that I respected tell me that I shouldn't do it. They told me that I should just evangelize. However, I knew what God had spoken into my spirit, so I kept moving forward with the direction of God. When we were in the storefront, I kept trying to work on a building fund, but every time I would begin to make progress something would happen to take the money. I asked God, why? Why can't I raise money for a building? He spoke to my spirit and told me he would provide the building and the money that I needed. I told someone close to me what God had spoken into my spirit. I told them God is going to give me a church. The person said, "you don't seriously think that someone is just going to give you a church do you?" I said yes, I do, because God told me he would. We have been in our new church now for about seven years. Along with the building we were given money to go towards a complete remodel. And God didn't stop there, he has also added three more pieces of property to the original. Once you have an experience of this kind of faith it becomes easier to believe for the next thing you are going to do. God builds your faith through each experience. Take a look at David. When he went to fight Goliath, he said when the bear came into my camp, the power of God came upon me and I killed him with my bare hands and the same thing happened when the lion came in, so this giant is nothing.

If you are getting ready to do something that is stretching your faith, just sit down and look back on other instances in your life where God moved for you, where he was faithful to you and encouraged you. Speak it out loud to God. Say, Lord, do you remember when you did this in my life and that in my life? In doing that you are reminding yourself. It builds your faith and then you can believe and rest in the knowledge that if he did it once he'll do it again. If you're worrying and stressing over it, it's not faith. That doesn't mean you never worry but in faith you pull from that assurance that you know that God is going to do it. Sometimes I wonder how or when but when faith kicks in, I know that he will do it in his way and in his time.

In Luke chapter 5, when Jesus saw a man being lowered down on a cot, he saw their faith, Acts chapter 3, when there was a paraplegic that needed to be healed, they said in Jesus' name, and it was the faith in the name of Jesus that made this man whole. Notice that in each of these examples, Jesus saw their faith, the man believed in Jesus and Paul perceived his faith. Now when it comes to the gift of faith, the minister can operate in that gift, or the person being prayed for can operate that gift. It's possible that if the minister doesn't feel the gift and the person being prayed for don't feel it, that the gift can rise up from the congregation. God will honor the faith of whoever is truly believing that, that thing which is being asked for is about to happen. In a congregational setting, three people are involved with the ability of the gift of faith. The person leading or the minister, the person being ministered to, and the congregation that is part of the ministry. It doesn't matter whose faith it is it is God that does the healing. In most cases someone operating in the gift of faith can move at any moment if they sense that gift of faith. No matter where the gift comes from man should never get the credit for what God does. It will happen for one reason and that is so that God will be glorified through his people.

Perry Stone shared a story about Oral Roberts early ministry when the great healing tent revivals were taking place. He had his tent set up in the Ohio Valley. They said people were being healed every night in the services and miracles were taking place. One night a mother carried her little girl, about 5 years old, up to him and told him that there were no bones in her lower leg and foot. The foot and leg were formed with muscles but there was no bone in them. No toe, ankle, nothing from the knee down. Brother Roberts told her, "Mom if this girl had a diseased bone or a broken bone I could pray, but she doesn't have a bone." And the mother said to Brother Roberts what kind of God do you serve anyway? You've been standing up there telling everybody that God can do the impossible. She said I am not asking you to heal her. I'm just asking you to pray, and God is going to heal her. Brother Roberts said, "Momma this will be off of your faith." He admitted that on that level of a creative miracle, he didn't have the faith. He said Lord, I'm going to do the praying, but this is on the momma. According to her faith so be it unto her. Remember Jesus made that statement, according to your faith, so be it unto you? And so, they end up praying and bone began to grow. They literally heard bones popping. A bone grew all the way down her leg into the foot and into her toes and that little girl for the first time in her life, when she was set down took off running around that tent. Brother Roberts lost total control of the service and had to dismiss and say you all shout and I will be back tomorrow night. A guy that was there that night, sitting on the front row said, thousands of people went crazy. People started jumping out of wheelchairs, throwing crutches, he said he didn't have to pray for anybody. Because when God did that miracle, faith hit everybody, and God will honor faith. When all the unbelief is out and it is pure one hundred percent faith, people can believe. God this is it. God, you can do it for me. It is supernatural. That is why it happens this way. So Oral Roberts admitted that he didn't have the faith needed that night, but the momma did. And that is not just faith but the gift of faith. She just believed. You know what, my daughter is walking out of here tonight with some bones in her legs.

The gift of faith is above the normal average miracle. Miracles and healings occur after the word is preached and after we pray because the word is what builds the faith, and the prayer is what touches the heart of God. In Hebrews it says, he likes to confirm his word with signs wonders and miracles of the Holy Ghost. Miracles are for the purpose of confirming and authenticating the word of God. The disciples said to Jesus in Luke 11:1, teach us how to pray. They didn't say teach us who to pray to, what to pray, or when to pray. Because they knew who to pray to, they had been doing it in the synagogue for years. They knew what to pray, because they had all kinds of prayers that they prayed in the synagogue. They didn't say teach us when to pray, because they already had set times to pray such as the ninth hour, three o clock in the afternoon they prayed. In the book of Acts you can see the disciples praying in line with the prayer times that were designated with the Jewish temple back in that day. Whether they are at the temple, whether they are at someone's home, they are praying at those designated times. But they said how do we pray? Now why did they say that? Because they saw prayers being prayed all the time by the pharisees and nothing was happening. No miracles were taking place. And they began to notice, hey when Jesus prays, something happens. So how does he pray to make this happen? The second thing the disciples ask Jesus is found in Luke 17:5 they say increase our faith. They knew that they believed but they also knew that faith can be increased. There is a faith you get the moment you are saved. Another level of faith that comes when you get the baptism of the holy ghost. There is another level of faith that comes when you start seeing miracles, and then you can believe for the miraculous.

There are four levels of faith found in the bible.

1. Little faith. In Matthew 14:31 when Peter is walking on the water, he took his eyes off Jesus and began to sink. Jesus rebuked him for having little faith. Now why did they have little faith. They had seen great miracles. They had seen the miracle of the loaves and fish multiplied. And then turned around and didn't have the faith for other things.

2. Simple faith. The woman said if she could touch the hem of Jesus garment she would be healed, Matthew 9:22. There was nothing great about it, nothing extraordinary, just I will go up and touch him and I know I will be made whole. Very simple faith.

3. Great faith. Then Matthew 15:28 says, there is great faith. The great faith is the gentile woman who sought healing for her daughter who is not present. And Jesus spoke healing to the daughter who was healed. And that was great faith.

4. So great faith. In the story of the centurion who was a commander of a group of a hundred roman soldiers. In this one he tells Jesus; my servant is sick but if you speak the word only, he will be healed. The bible says in psalms he sends forth his word and healed them and delivered them for all their destruction. So, there is the prophecy that the Lord will send his word to bring healing. It is not known if the centurion knew that passage, but he did recognize that Jesus had such authority over death, demons, and sickness that he knew that he didn't have to lay hands on anybody. He could just speak the word. And Jesus said, I have not seen so great a faith as this man has, because he is telling me just to speak the word. Everybody else is pulling him, lay your hands on my child, come to my house. My daughter just died; hurry get there. Mary and Martha, hey Lazarus is sick, you better hurry so you can heal him. Everybody else is wanting Jesus in person, but this guy says all you have to do is speak the word. This man understood. He had faith in the power of the word. How did he have faith? Because he had experience and knew what authority was. He said I can say to one man go there and he goeth. I can say to another man do this and he will do it. You have spiritual authority over this situation, speak the word. So, Jesus said, go thy way, they servant is healed. Now the servant was not where he could hear. He could have been a mile or more away and was in a house, yet when Jesus spoke the word, He got up off his death bed and was healed. God watches over his word and hastens to perform it.

So, you can have little faith. Probably when we first come to know the Lord, we don't know a lot, so we have little faith, and then our faith is simple. Simple faith is what our children have. When you tell a child something is going to happen, they believe something is going to happen. They look for it. They expect it. Then you bump your level of faith up to so great faith when you begin to understand the authority of the word.

In Hebrews chapter 11:1. NOW Faith is. We could say now I am going to the store. That means right now I am going to the store. It can imply that the way this is written faith is in the NOW. NOW faith is the substance. Not just faith is the substance of. . . But it is NOW. Activated faith is presently the substance of things hoped for, the evidence of thing not yet seen. So, faith can also sustain you with hope while you are waiting for a particular promise to be fulfilled. Jesus even said it this way. Even a small amount of faith can move a mountain. That mountain moving faith mentioned in the New Testament is a metaphor for moving a great problem in your life. Moving things out of your way. Something that is very important to know as we dig deeper in faith is its enemy. The greatest enemy of faith is unbelief. The greatest enemy of faith is doubt. It is very important to understand this. A fountain cannot produce bitter and sweet water at the same time. And a tree cannot produce fruit and thorns at the same time. There are many times when you find that people will pray for someone and immediately after they pray, they start talking contrary to their prayer. Well, we just have to keep praying. Keep holding to God and hopefully one day it will happen. It is contrary to what they just prayed. It is doubt and you have to know this. Miracles cannot happen where there is unbelief and doubt.

Example: Jesus from about the age of three or four till about the age of thirty is raised in a small town called Nazareth. The population during that time according to archeologist was probably around four hundred people. So, it was a small town. You had to go out of your way to go to Nazareth. It wasn't on a main thorough fare like the city of Galilee. Remember Nathanial said can any good thing come out of Nazareth. Jesus goes to the synagogue in Nazareth to preach and he preaches from the book of Isaiah, quoted in Luke 4:18. The spirit of the Lord is upon me, because he hath anointed me to preach the gospel to the poor; he hath sent me to heal the broken hearted, to preach deliverance to the captives, and recovering of sight to the blind, to set at liberty them that are bruised. To preach the acceptable year of the Lord. And he said today this scripture is fulfilled in your hearing and they get mad. They grab him and start pushing him, trying to push him off the edge of a cliff. He supernaturally walked through the midst of them and went his way, however he later comes back to this city to minister. This is his hometown. He is having miracles in other cities wherever he goes, but when he goes back to Nazareth, it says there he did no mighty miracles because of their unbelief. This is recorded in Mark 6:1-6. It says he laid his hands upon a few sick folks and healed them. It was because of their unbelief which means no faith. They did not have faith because they saw him only as the son of Mary and Joseph.

Unbelief is not having faith while doubt on the other hand is very similar, it is not as hard core as unbelief. Doubt can be persuaded to believe, whereas unbelief is just a no, I don't believe. The point is that doubt or unbelief will always hinder a person's faith and limit God's ability to intervene. Doubt and unbelief can be discerned by the spirit. Jesus could go into a place like Nazareth and knew they didn't have any faith and could do no mighty miracles. He could go to another town and see their faith and perform miracles. This is all recorded in the bible. Something important to note is that not only can the holy spirit discern when you believe but demons can discern whether or not you believe. When the disciples went to cast the devil out of that little epileptic boy, it says they could not cast it out. Jesus had to come and cast it out. Later the disciples asked Jesus, why couldn't we cast it out and he said because of your unbelief. The spirits in the boy had to know that the disciples weren't believing because it didn't leave the boy. The point I want to make is that demonic spirits can tell when you have faith and when you are in unbelief. Remember the seven sons of Sceva? When they went to cast demons out of a man, the demons said Jesus we know and Paul we know, but who are you? Faith must be involved in anything you are asking God for. You have to believe in order to be saved, with the heart man believes unto righteousness and with the mouth confession is made unto salvation. You have to believe to be baptized in the holy ghost. You have to believe for healing for miracles. Faith has to be involved in the operation of any gift of the spirit. God is not obligated if you do not believe.

The gift of faith enables the receiver to tap into the will of God to believe with increased confidence to pray with God's purpose to be accomplished. The gift of faith can also drive out the presence of unbelief or doubt. In other words when real faith comes, doubt leaves. Faith gives us a full assurance by the holy spirit that what we are praying for will be made evident.

The definition for the gift of faith is that it gives us supernatural confidence that God will do the thing that we ask. The gift of faith supernaturally increases the level of your expectancy. It also increases the level of faith in the heart of the receiver. When faith is present it can be sensed and increases the ability of other people to believe. It's very important that you understand that.

Faith is one of the three power gifts mentioned in 1 Corinthians 12:9-10. The power gifts are the working of miracles, the gifts of healing and faith. Faith is the first of the three power gifts mentioned and it is the strongest of the three. Without faith the other gifts cannot operate, so faith is a necessity. Faith is what generates the re-leasing of the power of God in a person or a situation.

There are three manifest expressions of faith. There is the measure of faith. There is the fruit of faith. There is the gift of faith. The measure of faith is an impartation given allowing a person to believe. The fruit of the faith in maturing in faith as you walk with God. The gift of faith is the impartation given to the believer to believe to the miraculous. All three of the measures of the level of faith are very important to understand.

Now we will look at the three levels as they are shown in scripture to see the difference in them. First let's look at Romans 12:3. For I say to the grace given unto me, to every man that is among you, not to think of himself more highly than he ought to think, but to think soberly, according as God hath dealt to every man the measure of faith. The Greek word measure means a portion or a certain degree. Every person has a certain measure of faith. You can prove this because the whole world is religious. The Hindus believe in their God. Islam believes in Allah. Jews believe in Jehovah. We Christians believe in God and in Jesus Christ. The whole world is religious. There is only a small percentage of the world that is completely pagan. That doesn't have some kind of God. Where does that idea come from? It comes from there being a measure of faith in everybody, although some are believing in the wrong type of God, there is something in them that makes them believe. There is a measure of faith in every human being. Some people through their unbelief destroy that measure. That is why you see atheist, agnostics, and unbelievers. According to the bible there is a measure of faith given to every person.

The fruit of faith. Galatians 5:22-23, but the fruit of the spirit is love, joy, peace, long suffering, gentleness, goodness, faith, meekness, temperance; against such there is no law. Notice that faith is listed in the fruit of the spirit. How does a person get faith as a fruit of the spirit? The answer is by the amount of word that you live by and that you know. When you study the word, you will automatically have a faith. It is not necessarily a gift of faith where you can believe for the miraculous, that is a supernatural gift. But if I asked if you have faith in the word, you would say yes, of course I do. Do you have faith to believe that Jesus is the son of God? Once again yes. Do you have faith that the holy spirit is real? Of course, I do. That is the fruit of faith your faith has matured like a tree or plant growing in your yard. You have the right amount of rain. The right amount of sun. You've been pruned every now and then. And now you are maturing, growing in the fruit of faith. Its automatic. You don't have to pray for it. You don't have to beg for it. You never have to ask for it because you are going to grow in your faith and knowledge of Jesus Christ both. It's a fruit. It automatically grows with you.

Then you have the gift of faith found in 1 Corinthians 12:9 to another faith by the same spirit: this is the supernatural ability to believe. When the gift of faith raises up in you it is a feeling, from the holy spirit, and you absolutely know that who you are praying for is about to get touched. It is overpowering. There is a difference between the gift and the fruit. The fruit of faith grows as you grow in the Lord, but the gift of faith is a supernatural impartation. In other words, one comes as you grow, just as fruit grows on a tree. You don't have to command an apple tree to produce apples, if it is healthy, when the season comes it will produce apples. It is the same thing with your faith. But the gift of faith is supernaturally imparted. The fruit of faith is a natural development by knowledge and understanding of God and the word. The more knowledge and understanding you have the more the fruit will emerge and develop in your life.

The gift of faith is imparted but works in line with the other gifts of the spirit. You cannot operate any of the other eight gifts unless there is a measure of faith. If you don't have faith, you won't have confidence. You will debate with yourself whether or not it is God speaking to you. Whether or not you should speak or move. If you don't have some measure of faith, you cannot operate in the other gifts. You do not have to have the gift of faith to operate in the other gifts, but you do have to have a measure of faith. It's good to have the gift of faith when being used in the gifts of working of miracles and healing, but you must have faith in order to step out and have confidence when you are flowing in the spirit.

Fruit should remain throughout your spiritual life but the gift while it is present, must be stirred up continually. In other word's if I follow God the fruit remains. It's there every day of your life. But when I have the gift of faith there are times, that I have to have a stirring up. Paul told Timothy "Do not neglect the gift that was given to you by the laying on of hands" then he turns right around and say's "stir up the gift." Rekindle the fire is what that phrase means. Don't neglect it, but you have neglected it so now you've got to stir it up. Sometimes the gift of faith has got to be stirred up

The fruit maintains an attitude of believing continually while the gift can be a sudden surge of faith to believe for the impossible. My fruit of faith means that I continually believe God. When I get up in the morning, I believe God will be with me today the same way he was yesterday. But the gift can suddenly come on you totally unannounced and unexpected in a situation where you need it. The fruit of faith is a possession, but the gift of faith is a manifestation. Peter had to receive the gift of faith to walk on water, because that is not an ordinary occurrence. He had to have trust in the word that Jesus said when he told him to come to him on the water, he had to have faith.

Now I will give you some examples of the gift of faith in operation. Acts 27 when Paul is on a boat going to go to Rome. He tries to tell the centurion and the guy running the boat, if we leave now, we are going to hit storms. But the centurion chose to trust the owner of the boat rather than Paul, so they set sail. In the journey they hit a storm called Euroclydon. The bible says that for fourteen days, the sun and moon did not appear. No stars. That's a disaster. That means they don't know where they are going in the ocean. For fourteen days they are throwing stuff off the boat including their food, trying to weather this storm. Paul said, all hope that we should be saved is taken from us. Now when Paul tells you that all hope is gone, you're in trouble. This is God's man. He knows faith. Then he said an angel of the Lord appeared to him and said Paul, here's what's going to happen. The ship is going to be destroyed but there will not be a loss any man's life. That is not only a word of knowledge, but it is also a faith builder for everyone else on that boat. This was a case where Paul could say, well, I have good news and bad news. The good news is we will all be spared. Don't anybody worry, I got a word from God, I have confidence in that word, and I have great faith that we will be okay. The bad news is the ship is going down. They floated to shore on broken pieces of the ship. That's how bad the storm was. The centurion wanted to kill all of the slaves because if they were to escape, he would be killed for allowing them to escape.

He was responsible for them. But the point here is that the apostle Paul got a word from God, and it triggered the gift of faith and he stood and prophesied to a whole boat of unbelieving men. Not only that but they ended up on an island and the whole island got saved.

Now here is something that you may not have caught in the story of Samson found in Judges 14-16. Samson has a Nazarite vow. His hair is long, in seven locks, which is part of the Nazarite vow. He goes down to the Philistine territory. And we all know that he lets Delilah mess with his hair. He has already broken two of his vows and this is the last one he's got to keep. He knows if he keeps messing around, he is going to lose the anointing of God. Each time Delilah says the Philistines be upon thee, he gets up with great confidence and takes the whole bunch on and whips them all. Each time he goes back to the same woman. Each time he gets up and beats them again. This happened a couple of times before he finally tells her the whole secret. Now think about this. The enemy is at the door, and he is sleeping. Why did he do that? Because he had confidence in the Nazarite vow and believed that God would be with him as long as he had is hair. Now this sounds like the opposite of what we think about Samson because he fell. But there was a faith that worked in him, that he could lay down and sleep, knowing that his enemy was right outside the door because he believed God would protect him. Did he go too far? Yes, he did. He broke the Nazarite vow. But he still didn't believe he would die, because even though the anointing was gone, he said I will shake myself as at other times before. He believed that he would keep the anointing. Now he was wrong, but the point is he had to have some kind of supernatural faith to even go in there in the first place. When he was asleep, they could have killed him any number of ways. Forget his hair. They could have stabbed him. They could have taken a spear and just run him through with it. But he somehow believes that he could stay right there, and nothing would happen. For him to do that he had to have a level of faith that we don't see, or the scripture does not tell us about. Obviously, the fact that he came back and defeated more enemies in his death than in his life; and the fact that in Hebrews 11:32-34 he is remembered in the list of heroes, tells you there is something that God feels about him that we don't pick up on.

The level of unbelief in people or an individual can hinder the operation of any gifts of the spirit. Matthew 13:54-57 says that Jesus' own family was offended at him because it says a prophet is without honor in his own country. Mark 6:5 says, he could do no mighty works or miracles because of their unbelief. He laid hands on a few sick folks, and they were healed. But it says he marveled because of their unbelief. We know that unbelief is the opposite of faith. But when the gift of faith rises up in you, it crushes the unbelief and doubt. Even in people with faith, the bible teaches us that your faith can fail you. In Luke chapter 22, Jesus tells Peter that he is going to deny the Lord three times. Peter says, I will not do that, I will go with you even to death. But Jesus says, no you're going to deny me three times. Watch what Jesus says, "but Peter, I'm going to pray for you that your faith will not fail." What does this mean about Peter's faith failing him? In other word's the situation was going to be so serious that if Jesus does not intercede, Peter's faith could totally fail. So not only does Jesus pray for God to bring him through this, but he also prays that his faith will not fail him in the midst of this huge test. The word fail in the Greek means to utterly fail or die. This word actually means to totally die out or to totally lose it all. What we would say today would be, I pray that you won't give up, quit, and just walk out of the ministry. Faith in Christ is a continuing process. You have to continually believe.

Jude 3 says that you have to contend for the faith that was once delivered to the saints. You can have right faith in the right thing which is the word of God and God himself. You can have wrong faith in the wrong thing. False doctrines false teachers, false religions. You can have wrong faith in the right thing. How can you do that? You should have confidence in people who love God, people who pray for you, or ministers. But don't put your faith in people. People who put their faith in people will eventually be disappointed by those people. It even says about Jesus that he didn't trust anybody because he knew what was in their hearts. They are yelling yay the Messiah, waving palm branches and four days later they are yelling crucify him. If you are in ministry, you will understand this. Oral Roberts made the statement to Ron Carpenter before he died, "Ron when you get to the end of your ministry if you can count three friends you've had in your life, who has not stabbed you in the back, betrayed you or talked about you behind your back you have done a great thing. It's okay to place confidence in people you trust but put your faith only in God. Keep your faith in Jesus Christ.

The gift of faith often works in co-operation with the gifts of working of miracles and healing. Both of these gifts occur often through the gift of faith. You should never abuse the gift of faith. 1 Timothy 2:6: Not be a novice lest being lifted up with pride you fall into the condemnation of the devil. The word novice here from the Greek means that which is newly planted. A plant with very shallow roots that can be easily overturned in a slight storm. It does not mean one that is young in years but one that is young in the faith. Age has nothing to do with spiritual maturity. It comes from prayer, study, and seeking God. I've seen many younger people being used by the Lord in many ways, whether in preaching or in the gifts because they apply themselves in learning. But it doesn't come over night. Spiritual maturity takes time to develop. It's according to how much you apply yourself in your relationship with the Lord. That's why it is not wise to put someone into an office in the church right after they get saved. They need time to grow and develop their walk with God. They need to be encouraged in the word and in their growth. We also need to understand that not everybody in the church is saved and sanctified. Not everybody is working on spiritual growth at the same speed.

A good example of not abusing your faith is James and John, known as the sons of thunder. They were the sons of Zebedee, and they owned a fishing business. Jesus gave them the nickname in Mark 3:17. He gave surnames to many of his disciples. Simon was called Peter. James and John were called the sons of thunder. In Luke 9:54-55, James and John got angry and they wanted to call fire down on the city of Samaria and burn everybody up. Now this brings a complicated theological question. If the prophet Elijah could call fire down on Mount Carmel through his prayer, would it be possible that Jesus or his disciples could have the authority to fire down from God out of heave? Theoretically it would be possible, but Jesus would never allow it to happen. Jesus told them that they didn't know what manner of spirit they were of. They wanted to abuse their faith, they wanted to use their faith for a wrong motive.

What if Jesus would have said, ok go ahead and burn the whole place? Everybody in Samaria would have died. They would have missed, this same John in Acts chapter 8, who goes down to the city of Samaria to lay hands on the brand-new Samaritan converts and they all received the baptism of the Holy Ghost. So, God did send fire, but it wasn't a natural fire. It was the fire of the Holy Ghost. So, aren't you glad that God doesn't answer every prayer that you pray? Or I should say doesn't answer the way that you want him to. God knows what lays ahead of us and what we are asking for today, may not be good for us tomorrow.

You cannot fake faith. Either it's there or it's not there. Here are some of the benefits of having the gift of faith in operation. The gift of faith in operation is needed to experience a miracle. It helps you to be able to believe that when you pray that the miracle can actually happen. The gift of faith works with the gift of healing. A minister has to believe, or the person being prayed for has to believe or the congregation present must believe. Somebody has got to be believing. The gift of faith doesn't tell you God can, it tells you that God will. You can sense it while you are praying, that God is doing what you are asking. You can feel it in your spirit. Also, the gift of faith is used for people to receive the baptism in the Holy Ghost. There is a gift of laying on of hands for receiving the Holy Ghost. In Acts chapter 8 as I mentioned before Phillip preached salvation to people and many were being saved but Peter and John came and laid hands on them and they received the Holy Ghost. In Acts 8:17 it says, and Peter laid hands on them, and they received the Holy Ghost. Paul did the same thing to a group of disciples. Acts 19:6 Ananias, who was a deacon in the church, not an apostle. When God spoke to him to go lay hands-on Saul after his conversion in Acts 9:17, Ananias said receive your sight brother and be filled with the Holy Ghost, and it happened.

It is important that you remain in the gifts that you have been gifted with. If a person for example has the gift of healing and you are having a prayer line for the sick, the person with that gift needs to be praying for people. They have a special anointing for that purpose and that is where their faith is strongest. There is a grace for every gift. Just as people are gifted in the area of their call, such as being called to be a pastor, an evangelist, a missionary whatever God has called you to he gifts you and gives you grace for that calling. He does this also in the gifts of the spirit. One may be used more in the gift of healing where another may flow more in the gift of prophecy. You need to walk in your gifting and be obedient to the spirit that moves through you.

Remember that faith is a fruit, but it is also a gift. There are levels of faith, from little faith to great faith. The gift can be desired and prayed for. In Corinthians, Paul said covet earnestly the best gift. Why would he say covet earnestly the best gift? If we take the English word covet, we tend to see it as being negative, because one of the ten commandments is, thou shalt not covet. But this is why we need to do word studies. Here the word covet means to strongly desire in a positive sense. So, in other words, strongly desire the best gift. What is the best gift? The best gift is the gift that is needed for that situation. Because if you are standing in front of someone who is dying, they don't necessarily need discerning of spirits. They don't need you to discern anything, they are dying. What they need is a miracle. You may be standing in front of someone who has a crisis on their hands. They don't need healing; they may need a word of knowledge. So, the best gift is the gift needed at that time. The gifts can be desired and obtained through prayer. Paul said to Timothy stir up the gift that was given you by the laying on of hands. It is true that some gifts can come through laying of hands. When you are around giftings, those gifts can be imparted to you.

Numbers 11:

24. And Moses went out, and told the people the words of the LORD, and gathered the seventy men of the elders of the people and set them round about the tabernacle.

25. And the LORD came down in a cloud, and spake unto him, and took of the spirit that was upon him, and gave it unto the seventy elders: and it came to pass that when the spirit rested upon them, they prophesied, and did not cease.

26. But there remained two of the men in the camp, the name of the one was Eldad, and the other Medad: and the spirit rested upon them; and they were of them that were written but went not out unto the tabernacle: and they prophesied in the camp.

27. And there ran a young man, and told Moses and said, Eldad and Medad do prophesy in the camp.

28. And Joshua the son of Nun, the servant of Moses, one of his young men, answer and said, my lord Moses, forbid them.

29. And Moses said unto him, enviest thou for my sake? Would God that all the LORD'S people were prophets, and that the LORD would put his spirit upon them!

Deuteronomy 34:9, And Joshua the son of Nun was full of the spirit of wisdom; for Moses had laid his hands upon him: and the children of Israel hearkened unto him and did as the Lord commanded Moses.

1 Samuel 10:11, And it came to pass when all that knew him before time saw that, behold, he prophesied among the prophets, then the people said one to another, what is this that is come unto the son of Kish? Is Saul also among the prophets.

1 Samuel 19:20, And Saul sent messengers to take David, and when they saw the company of the prophets prophesying, and Samuel standing as appointed over them, the Spirit of God was upon the messengers of Saul, and they also prophesied.

THE VOCAL GIFTS

Diverse Tongues
Interpretation of Tongues
Prophecy

DIVERSE TONGUES

Diverse or different kinds of tongues.

1 CORINTHIANS 14:1-2, FOLLOW AFTER CHARITY, AND DESIRE spiritual gifts, but rather that ye may prophesy. For he that speaketh in an unknown tongue speaketh not unto men, but unto God: for no man uderstandeth him; howbeit in the spirit he speaketh mysteries.

Notice here that it calls the tongue an unknown tongue. Unknown is in italics in most verses and that means it is not in the original Greek text but, in a translation, sometimes you are required to put (for example in the English bible) certain words to make it a complete statement as far as the English grammar is concerned. If we read, he that speaketh in a tongue, we could say that just refers to languages back in that day. When it says, he that speaketh in the unknown tongue, we know that it is referring to the operation of a gift of the Holy Spirit. So unknown is going to be used in the translation to emphasize that it is a language that is not known to the speaker.

Every denomination in America and in the west has always had one particular doctrine that became their foundation or focal point of their denomination. If we go back through history, we have the Lutherans whose emphasis was justification by faith. Martin Luther said the just shall live by faith. So, it re-established faith in the blood of Christ.

Later came the Methodist. These would be for example the

Wesley brothers or Wesleyan Methodist and their big emphasis in their time was sanctification. Their doctrinal emphasis was separation. They noticed that people were being saved by faith, but their lives were not changing. They still had the old nature. So, they brought in sanctification, saying, you need to be sanctified so that your habits, your conversation, your walk changes. So, sanctification became a very strong doctrine. Especially with the Wesleyan Methodist but with the Methodist in general.

Then we have the Baptist. The Baptist were actually very early so I am not putting them in order. The Baptist presented baptism after salvation. So, their roots can be traced back to that time frame and water baptism. Be saved be baptized in water. The Baptist do not wait for water baptism. There are a lot of churches that don't even talk about baptism, but Jesus said to repent and be baptized. The Baptist have kept this teaching very much alive as they should have, and all other churches really should as well.

Pentecostal began to emphasize the outpouring of the Holy Spirit. The Murphy outpouring in 1898. The Isuzu Street outpouring in 1906. And the Topeka Kansas outpouring in the year 1900. They began to emphasize the nine gifts of the spirit, but they also began putting emphasis on speaking in tongues as the initial evidence of the Holy Spirit.

The Charismatic was on worship. If you know anything about the charismatic movement, they are the ones that introduced the Praise Team. The Baptist, Pentecostal and Methodist churches had the robed choirs. The Charismatic Church came out with a bunch of kinds singing with a band and drums telling everybody to get up off their seat and start worshipping. So, what you see today with praise and worship teams, standing up and reading from a screen actually has its original roots in the charismatic renewal whose emphasis was worshipping God.

Everyone has similar beliefs as far as the major denominations. Most believe in the Holy Spirit. Most believe that the Holy Spirit is part of the triune God head. The only people who differ with that would be the UPC (United Pentecostal Church), and they believe that God is Jesus; that the Holy Spirit is God and there is only one who manifest in those three ways. But most believe in the trinity. The evangelicals believe in the trinity. Most denominations baptize in the name of the father, son, and Holy Ghost. The one who does not baptize that way is the UPC and they baptize in the name of Jesus only.

Most believe in the biblical manifestation of the Holy Spirit. If we were to divide all of the mainline denominations whether they would be the Baptist or the Lutherans, or the Methodist, or Presbyterians, Episcopalians. If we put those in one group and in another group, we would place your eight major Pentecostal denominations and your three or four major charismatic denomination. And we put the mainline denominations in a bundle themselves. Here are the three main divisions. There is a division on the work of the Holy Spirit in our time.

Meaning, does the Holy Spirit only convict of sin and comfort people? Does the Holy Spirit not only convict of sin and bring people to Jesus? Does the Holy Spirit manifest in different forms such as the manifestations of gifts?

The second major division is in the operation of the nine gifts. Are they valid today? Are only some valid today or have all been done away with? This is a factor that many of the mainline denominations if you look at how they view Pentecostals and Charismatics.

The third major difference would be the operation of the gift of speaking in tongues. This is probably the greatest division. Some questions around the gift of tongues are, is it valid today? If it is valid how and why is it valid? What are these seven hundred and eighty million spirit baptized people around the world doing who claim to be speaking in some kind of a supernatural prayer language? The biggest division in the body of Christ is over one issue. It is not in how we worship. A lot of the denominations today are clapping their hands and raising their hands and praising the Lord. The issue is speaking in other tongues. There are churches that teach that it does not exist today. They say it is not necessary today, or if you pray in English why would you even want to pray in another language.

Let's take a look at the New Testament terms that are used. Jesus first introduces the fact in Mark 16:17 when he is giving final instructions to his disciples, and he told them that they would speak with new tongues. He didn't say unknown tongues here, because as I said before the word unknown is in italics identifying that it is not known to the speaker, but here Jesus said it would be a brand-new tongue. The Lord promised in the Old Testament he would give people a new heart; he would put a new spirit in them; he would create in them a new mind; and here he talks about new tongues. So, this is a new language that his disciples are going to be able to pray in. Then we find in Acts 2:4, and they were all filled with the Holy Ghost, and began to speak with other tongues, as the spirit gave utterance. This happened during the festival of Pentecost. Notice it says that they ALL began to speak in other tongues as the Holy Spirit gave them utterance. In Acts 10:44, while Peter yet spoke these words, the Holy Ghost fell on all of them which heard the word; v.45 And they of the circumcision which believed were astonished, as many as came with Peter, because that on the Gentiles also was poured out the gift of the holy Ghost. v.46 for they heard them speak with tongues and magnify God.

Jude 20 says; But ye, beloved, building up yourselves on your most holy faith, praying in the Holy Ghost. This let's s know that we are building up our faith when we are praying in the Holy Ghost.

1 Corinthians 14:15; What is it then? I will pray with the spirit, and I will pray with the understanding also: I will sing with the spirit, and I will sing with the understanding also. Here Paul is dealing with the gift of tongues and when he says praying with the Spirit, He is talking about praying in the prayer language or praying in tongues.

So basically, your terms are new tongues; speaking in other tongues; speaking with tongues; praying in the Holy Ghost; and praying in the Spirit. Each of these basic terms mean the same thing and in each of these instances it would refer to the initial moment a person is baptized in the Holy Spirit, in its fullness and they speak in the prayer language, and they speak with the new tongue. All though the terms are different they all refer to that action. The first group of Jews were filled on the day of Pentecost in Acts 2. The first group of Gentiles in Acts 10. Jude talks about praying with the Spirit. He is talking to a group of people that believe in the Spirit and have received the Spirit so now he is talking to them about praying in the Spirit. This is the prediction of the evidence of tongues. It is where it first happened among the Jews and then where it first happened among the Gentiles. And the other references tie into the benefits of speaking with other tongues. All of this happens, in the bible, when a person is first baptized in the Holy Spirit.

So, let's go to the ideas of why we believe that speaking in other tongues is evidence. In the bible it is recorded as the first evidence of Holy Ghost baptism. We are going to talk about the outpouring and those that received it. In Acts 2:1-4, there are one hundred and twenty believers that it specifically says when they were filled with the Holy Spirit they spoke in tongues as the Spirit gave utterance. They knew they were filled. They knew they were fulfilling the words of Jesus speaking with new tongues because, why? The spirit spoke through them. In the city of Samaria, Acts 17, they are laying hands upon them to receive the Holy Spirit, and this was an outpouring that was so powerful that a sorcerer wanted to have that same anointing that Peter and John had to lay hands on people and for them to receive the Holy Spirit. Then in Acts 9:17 we see, not an outpouring, but a man saying to Saul receive your sight and be filled with the Holy Spirit and we know that he spoke in tongues in 1 Corinthians chapter 14. This one man's baptism in the Holy Spirit led to the outpouring of the Holy Spirit to the whole Gentile branch of the church.

So, we see a city receiving; a household receiving; a limited number of disciples receiving, but with Paul it was not just one believer being filled but this would lead to the whole Gentile movement.

Cornelius' household we don't know how many received but according to the word, it was an entire house filled with people, and when they were filled; they all spoke with tongues. Acts 19:1-7 says they all spoke with tongues as the spirit gave utterance. The one common link is that they spoke in other tongues. Meaning that if we look simply at the New Testament, that the first evidence of a person knowing that they have been baptized in the Holy Spirit with the enduement of power, the very first evidence in every reference is the manifestation out of their mouth. The overflow comes with God's power, and they begin to speak with other tongues. Speaking with other tongues is called, *Glossolalia*. From *Glosso* which means the tongue and *lalia* which means the language. Meaning to talk in a language or to speak in other tongues. The term unknown tongues again, mentioned in 1 Corinthians 14:2, 4, 13, 14, 17 & 19, showing that the language was unknown to the speaker.

Why should a believer have a desire to speak in divers' kinds of tongues? This is a question that is often asked by other denominations that does not believe this gift is for us today. First of all, what are diver's kind of tongues? These are actual languages. They are both known languages which are civilized; and they can also be primitive forms of languages that does not exist except maybe in a few parts of the world. Paul also said in 1 Corinthians 13:1 that these can be the tongue of angels. So, there are heavenly tongues and there are earthly tongues. There are known languages and there are unknown languages. There are still languages maybe in the jungles or in the mountains of Africa that we may not have quite tapped into yet.

Perry Stone talked about a time very early in his ministry when, while preaching he began to speak in tongues. It was a completely different language. There was a lady there that recorded it. She took the recording to a man who was a professor of Indian artifacts. He was an archeologist who dealt specifically with Indian artifacts. He was working through Radford University, but he was from Syria. Now when the lady took the cassette tape of Perry speaking in tongues, she said I would like to know what language this man is speaking. The professor translated what he was saying from an old form of Chaldean Aramaic. He said this particular form of the language is so old that only a few people in Syria speak it. It is not spoken most places in the world, and I can speak it because my family is from Syria. He thought that Perry was a Jewish Rabbi giving a lecture. When she told him that it was a twenty-two-year-old preacher that didn't know any language except English, he was completely stunned. Later the Lord actually appeared to this man supernaturally, about two months later in a snowstorm, and he accepted the Lord as his Savior. So, there can be known languages; Chinese; Japanese; Portuguese; Spanish; English etc. That many people speak and there can be languages that are old languages, that have practically died that the Holy Spirit still knows, and a person can speak it. This is unknown. Why is it unknown? Because it is unknown to you. You are not sure what you are saying it is the spirit praying through you.

Divers' kind of tongues are interesting because on the day of Pentecost approximately sixteen nations found in Acts 2:8-11, heard these Galileans speaking in their own tongues. They were amazed, they were in doubt, they were asking what meaneth this? The answer was that this was the wonderful, wonderful works of God. Some believe that the gift of tongues restores the voice of God on earth to a generation that has been assaulted by the powers of the enemy. It is very significant that we understand that we are in a very great crisis in our country. The whole world is about to go into a crisis, and we have to have the spirit and we must be able to pray in the spirit and know the mind of the spirit.

Speaking with tongues is going to become very significant when you understand what Paul wrote about the significance of having this gift and the purpose of this gift in the life of a believer.

So we go to the question, why should we speak in tongues? Again, there are what the bible calls divers' kinds of tongues. There are numerous benefits with this gift. Isaiah 28:11-12: For with stammering lips and another tongue he will speak to his people.

To whom he said, this is the rest wherewith ye may cause the weary to rest; and this is the refreshing; yet they would not hear. It is important to understand this verse because this verse of stammering lips and another tongue God will speak unto his people is referred to by the apostle Paul in his letter to the church at Corinth. Paul quotes the part where it says with stammering lips and another tongue God speaks to his people but the part that Isaiah emphasizes here, remember there was no speaking with another tongue in Isaiah's day, but he emphasizes this is the rest wherein you may cause the weary to rest and this is the refreshing. In other words, he is saying here that this gift, when we go to 1 Corinthians 14, is a prophecy that deals with speaking in tongues. That the baptism in the Holy Spirit and the speaking in tongues brings a rest into a person's spirit and it brings a refreshing.

Those who operate in this gift knows that when you get alone with God, and you pray in what we call the prayer language it brings a refreshing to you. That is why you can go into church totally exhausted and say I don't know if I can make it through the service but when the spirit of God shows up you leave totally alert and awake. It's very difficult to explain that unless you understand it is because the Holy Spirit brings rest to the weary and the Holy Spirit will bring refreshing.

There is also an emotional benefit to speaking with tongues. Romans 8:26-27 says, Likewise the Spirit also helpeth our infirmities: for we know not what we should pray for as we ought: but the Spirit itself maketh intercession for us with groanings which cannot be uttered. 27. And he that searcheth the hearts knoweth what is the mind of the Spirit, because he maketh intercession for the saints according to the will of God. Now notice this, that we don't know what to pray for. How many times has someone presented a vague request, for example they might say, pray God will show me where to move? How do we pray for that? Should we pray for them to move out of town? Should we pray for them to move in town? We need to be specific and sometimes we don't know what to pray for.

But the bible says that the Spirit will make intercession. And that word intercession actually means in Greek, to take hold of together with. It means two people taking hold of something together. So, the Holy Spirit takes hold of your situation while you are praying and stands in the gap for you with groanings that cannot be uttered. Groaning can be referred to as inarticulate speech. A speech that you cannot articulate on your own. Articulate means to voice or speak fluently. If you are familiar with the old-time prayer warriors, one of the things that they would do is they would groan in the Spirit.

There are times that we may get frustrated with a situation, maybe we feel some guilt, we have doubts, we are not sure how to pray about a situation, so Romans 8 says the Spirit makes intercession for us.

Here is what Paul taught. 1 Corinthians 14:14; For if I pray in an unknown tongue, my spirit prayeth, but my understanding is unfruitful. We are a three part being 1 Thessalonians 5:23 tells us we are a body, a soul, and a spirit. The flesh man operates on five senses: hearing, seeing, smelling, tasting, and touching. God uses those five senses to speak to us. The first spiritual benefit of praying in the Spirit is our spirit is praying but my understanding is unfruitful. Our understanding is not benefited by it. It does not produce. So why is it necessary for our spirit to pray if we don't understand. Think about this. This has happened to me a lot of times. I can be praying for someone, and I don't necessarily know what they need, but God (the Holy Ghost) knows exactly what they need. The spirit will take over and I will begin to pray in tongues for what they need. I don't need to know but the spirit can make the intercession for me. Maybe someone tells you, I need prayer because I am in stage four cancer. If you begin to pray for that person in the English language, it is possible for your mind to say, oh boy, stage four. That's really bad. You know sister Jones died with that a year ago. Remember that other lady ten years ago? She had stage four to. Your intellect is a memory bank and in that memory bank is both good and bad memories. Your flesh man, when you are trying to pray for certain difficult things, will kick into that memory bank, and instead of pulling out, God healed someone of that thirty years ago, or I remember reading a book about that man that got healed, your flesh man will pull out the negative. This is the instinct of the carnal man, to be negative. So, suddenly you are getting all of these negative thoughts and you are trying to pray but you are not believing what you are praying for. When you start praying in the Holy Ghost you start feeling the anointing and faith rise up inside of you. Speaking in tongues bypasses your understanding and you can't go into unbelief when you are praying in the Holy Ghost. You are praying according to Romans 8, the will of God. There is a reason God said there is a benefit of your spirit praying and your intellect mind not being fruitful or not totally understanding.

The second thing that we have to understand is that sometimes we do not know what to pray for. Romans 8:26-27, Likewise the Spirit also helpeth our infirmities: (this word is translated weakness in the NKJV, and it means weakness of mental, spiritual, emotional, any kind of weakness) for we know not what we should pray for as we ought: but the Spirit itself maketh intercession for us with groanings which cannot be uttered. 27. And he that searcheth the hearts knoweth what is the mind of the Spirit, because he maketh intercession for the saints according to the will of God.

That word groaning means to sigh. It actually comes from a word that means to mutter, to mumble, to pray inaudibly. The root word in the word groanings is used for grief. Like an internal feeling, such as someone groaning in sorrow or grief of some sort. The Spirit prays for us when we are heavy hearted, when we are burdened, and we are not sure what to pray for. That's when the spirit man through the Holy Spirit in you kicks in. Part of the mystery of how the human body is made is you are a body, soul, and spirit. Now if you were to die your vocal cords, your larynx, your voice box, your windpipe, and your tongue all things needed to communicate audibly are still in your body. However, if your spirit were to come out of your body and go to either heaven or hell, it still can talk. The rich man in hell could communicate. Abraham in paradise could communicate. The beggar could communicate. How could they do it? They could see, they saw each other. They could hear they could feel because the man in hell said I am in pain. They had memory. All the senses still work outside of your body. Why is it important to understand that? When I am baptized in the Holy Spirit and I have the prayer language and I begin to speak with other tongues, I am using all of my natural facilities for that word to be formed. My mouth, my tongue has to form the words. My voice, the air has to come over my vocal cords for me to be able to speak. So, I am using everything natural to produce the sound of that tongue God has given me but here is the key, it is coming out of my spirit and not out of my head. That's why there is power when you speak it. Because the anointing abides in you. The bible says in John 7, out of your belly will flow rivers of living water. The spirit of man is the candle of the Lord searching all the inner parts of the belly according to the book of Proverbs. So, from our inner most being the spirit is flowing out of us, and yet it requires all of the senses, all of the organs of our human body that God gave us to communicate with, it requires all of them to speak in tongues.

Usually before you speak in tongues you will hear yourself speaking in tongues in your mind first. That is why many times people will thing they are doing it on their own or that they are making it up in their mind. But if you will trust the Lord and begin to speak what you are hearing in your mind the spirit will take over and you will begin to speak in tongues. The Holy Spirit gives your spirit the words. You are hearing your spirit praying in your mind, you are just not speaking it with your mouth. So, when you decide to trust the Lord and speak what is in your mind, you are giving voice to your spirit. That is why it says in Acts they spoke as the spirit gave them utterance. He is giving them the words, but they had to do the speaking. So, in the gift of the Holy Spirit, the Holy Spirit is there. The Spirit of the Lord is there. It is already in your spirit once you have received, but you have to be obedient to use the physical aspect of the tongue and the vocal cords and those things necessary for you to be able to communicate it.

Now the third reason. For he that speaketh in an unknown tongue speaks not unto men, but unto God: for no man understandeth him; howbeit in the spirit he speaketh mysteries (2 Corinthians 14:2). Concerning speaking mysteries, it could mean mysteries about the plans of God; mysteries about your future; things that you don't understand. So, the idea of speaking mysteries is very broad. When a preacher puts together a message to be preached, or a singer writes a song. Anything related to ministry. When the person prays for that area of ministry or to know how to do something, God will begin to show you what you need to know. That is mysteries being revealed. You can unlock hidden things in the kingdom when you pray in the Holy Spirit. God will give you revelations of things that are going to take place so that you can prepare for them. He will give you visions. He will let you know things that you need to know if you are praying about those things.

Now the fourth reason is to build our faith. Jude 20 says: But ye beloved building up yourselves on your most holy faith, praying in the Holy Ghost. Building up is the same word used for edifying. In this point we are building up our faith. How can we build our faith? According to Jude, we can build it by praying in the Holy Spirit. The Holy Spirit builds up and energizes you, like a battery. Literally like a battery. If the battery gets low the Holy Spirit builds it up. It is the energy and life that we call the anointing. It begins to expand in your heart, it expands in your mind, and it expands in your spirit. As it does you begin to get another level of faith that you did not have before.

Another reason or benefit for speaking in tongues is in Acts 10:46 where it says, they spoke with tongues and magnified God. When you speak in tongues, you magnify God. Now we know that God is God. God can be no greater than He already is because He is already great. He will be no more powerful than He already is because He is already all powerful. When you speak in tongues you magnify the size of God in your eyes. Suddenly He is greater than you thought He was, He is bigger than you thought He was. He is stronger than you thought He was. So, one of the other reasons for speaking in tongues is to magnify God.

There are different uses or diverse uses for tongues. These are the five basic benefits for the gift of tongues. These are the types, the different uses for the gift of tongues. One is 1 Corinthians 14:2, we are speaking to God in tongues, but our understanding is unfruitful, that is used in devotional tongues. The church at Corinth was a church that operated very heavily in speaking in tongues, but Paul said I speak in tongues more than all of you. Now this is a tongue talking church and Paul is having to correct them on some of their abuses. But how does he do it? He doesn't do it when speaking. People that are against speaking in tongues will tell you, Paul said when speaking in the church he would rather speak five words of his own language than to speak ten thousand words in an unknown tongue. But they don't read the rest of it. That by my voice I might teach others also. What Paul was saying is I'm not going to stand behind the pulpit and preach in tongues. You won't understand it. You won't know what I'm saying. It will not edify you. I am speaking in my own language because I want to teach you something. So, when Paul said I speak in tongues more than you all, he was not speaking of a church service but of a devotional time. Private prayer time tongues. When I pray between me and God tongues.

Then there are revelatory tongues. 1 Corinthians 14:2, revealing mysteries. God will give you revelation of His Word. He will open it to you. As a preacher I will say it is amazing to me how God will give me a message and let me see things in His word that I have read many times before but did not see.

There are tongues for edification. You edify yourself when you pray in tongues. Jude said building up yourself in the faith. So, you are constantly building up your inner man or your spirit by praying in tongues. 1 Corinthians 14:2 says that tongues are a sign to the unbeliever. How are they a sign to the unbeliever? This is where divers' kinds of tongues come in. There is a difference in baptismal tongues and divers' tongues. Baptismal tongues are the one that you are given when you get baptized in the Holy Spirit. This is the tongue that you pray in regularly. Divers' tongues mean different types of tongues. Usually when you begin to pray more frequently in tongues you will move into a different realm, and you will begin to hear a different sound or a different type of tongue. Why would there be a need for different types of tongues. They can be used as a sign to the unbeliever. I am using Perry Stones example on this one, but I have heard testimonies of other times that this has happened. Perry Stone said that his uncle Rufus, who only had a third-grade education and never took lessons in any other languages. could go up to someone of another nationality or culture and speak their language fluently. He had the baptismal tongue from when he first got saved. But divers' tongues came after that, and God used it as a sign to the unbeliever when he could speak to them in their language. The sign to the unbeliever is one of the great reasons that God allows you to operate in divers' tongues. I have heard testimonies where someone prayed or gave a message in a tongue that happened to be the language of a visitor that was in the congregation that day and the visitor understood it perfectly, because it was their language, even though the person speaking had no idea what they were saying. We are not on interpretation right now but when a person gives a message in tongues and there is a person who speaks that language in the congregation it does not need to be interpreted because that person got the message. They have received the message.

Tongues are also used in worship because Paul said I will sing in the spirit and sing with the understanding also. We have seen this happen when people will begin to sing in tongues. It is a most remarkable thing. I have seen it happen several times. The person will be singing a song and suddenly, they will begin to sing in tongues. The music does not change. The rhythm is the same, but the words are unknown. When this happens, it changes the atmosphere to one of reverence and worship toward God.

So, to sum up, the gift of tongues is separate from the tongue that is given when you are initially baptized in the Holy Spirit. In the baptism it is one single language. In divers' tongues it is multiple languages. Not everyone has the gift of tongues, but everyone can receive the baptism of the Holy Spirit according to Acts 2:38.

The gift of tongues often involves actual languages such as what occurred when the Spirit was poured out on the day of Pentecost. When you have the baptismal tongue sometimes it doesn't even sound like a language. If you hear some people only have two or three or four words that they say. They might be saying glory to God. They might be saying God is Great. They are saying just a few words. When you have divers' tongues it is an actual fluent language of some type, and the grammar is perfect. The gift of tongues when used in a public service is given to be interpreted. We will deal with this in the interpretation of tongues.

The more you pray in the spirit and use the prayer language God gave you when you received the baptism the more the possibility is of divers' tongues operating in your life.

Remember that when you pray in tongues it is the Spirit praying for you making intercession. You might be in an area of warfare and the Holy Spirit wants to change the payer language for whatever reason and that is why you change from one form of language to another. When you go into divers' kinds of tongues many times it can be used to witness to a person who speaks that language or is possibly going to be connected in a mission field or area where that language is spoken.

The diver's kind of tongues needs no interpretation. On Pentecost there is no interpretation. They are all speaking in tongues but there are sixteen different languages', and they all understand what they are saying, so they are receiving the message. There is no necessity of an interpretation when the message is being received.

Everyone needs the baptism of the Holy Spirit and let's go back to the original thought, covet earnestly the best gift, and that is the gift that is needed for that moment. Don't ever be afraid to let the Holy Spirit change the prayer language because there could be a reason for it that you might not be aware of.

THE GIFT OF INTERPRETATION
OF TONGUES

WE HAVE STUDIED ABOUT THE GIFT OF TONGUES AND THE difference between the tongue given at the point of baptism and the gift of divers' tongues. The gift of tongues given at the point of baptism is known as the prayer language, but the gift of divers' tongues is used in different ways. They can be used as a supernatural sign to people in a congregation. One reason is to reach the unbeliever or sometimes God wants to bring a message through his people to his church to edify the body. He will use it through a prophetic utterance or as Paul says through a tongue and interpretation of that particular tongue.

1 Corinthians 14:4-5 says, He that speaketh in an unknown tongue edifieth himself; but he that prophesieth edifieth the church. 5. I would that ye all spake with tongues, but rather that ye prophesied: for greater is he that prophesieth than he that speaketh with tongues, except he interprets, that the church may receive edifying.

What is happening here is that many of those in this church have received the baptism of the Holy Spirit and they speak with tongues. They are worshipping in tongues. According to Paul they have been singing in tongues. They really love this gift, and they are having a great time but what Paul tells them is basically they are edifying themselves. He says now to edify the church we need a prophetic word that everybody can hear. Or we need a message in tongues that is interpreted so that everybody in the church can be edified. Then he gives rules and order for how many times a message should be given, and an interpretation should be given. So that you don't end up with a whole service where everybody is speaking in tongues and trying to interpret.

The emphasis here is not trying to push one gift over the other and putting down speaking in tongues. What he is saying is this, if all of you simply edify yourself the whole time that is great, but if someone can give an edification exhortation comfort through a prophetic word, meaning the preaching of the word from the word. Keep in mind that they only had the Old Testament to preach from, they did not have the New Testament to preach from like we do now. But they could get up and talk about Jesus. They could share testimonies of what Jesus had done and was doing for either themselves or people they knew. This is edification. Paul was telling them that they had to edify the church meaning the entire body. He say's here is what you need to do. If you are going to speak in a tongue out loud, let someone give an interpretation for the purpose of benefiting those that are in the congregation. Since speaking in tongues is an unknown tongue there are times when the tongue should be interpreted. This is especially true if the tongue is spoken in a public setting such as what we call a message from the Holy Spirit.

First let us talk about what this gift is not. This gift is not an educated person interpreting a known language that is present. That is simply an interpreter. Usually someone is trained to do that. Those types of interpreters are used on the mission fields for example.

This gift is not reading the bible in Greek then interpreting it to the congregation in their language. Some people have tried to imply that is what Paul is talking about when he wrote this. The New Testament was written in the Greek language, and it did have to be interpreted from the letter Paul wrote to the congregation but that is not the supernatural gift of interpretation, that is just an ability someone has to give the interpretation to a letter.

It is not learning a language of how to speak those words and what those words mean. It not taking a Hebrew class and learning how to read Hebrew, and then saying, now I can interpret that language.

The gift of interpreting tongues is very significant because it is a supernatural gift where God inspires an individual to speak out loud so everybody can hear, a message in an unknown tongue and then someone with the gift, interpreting that for the ears of the congregation.

In 1 Corinthians chapter 12 and verse 30 it says, not all have the gift to interpret. But we are told that a person should seek the ability to interpret. To interpret a tongue demonstrates a sign and wonder of the Holy Spirit within the church and within the body of Christ. When speaking in tongues, there are private devotional tongues and then there are what we call public messages in tongues. A private devotional tongue is used in speaking directly to God and that can happen in any church service. Paul said let him that speaks in the tongue however pray that he may interpret. So, we know that in the bible Paul said if there be no interpreter then let the person speak to themselves and to God. What does that mean? Private tongues remain quieter. You are bearing your heart to God. Then there is what's called public messages in tongues. With this tongue the voice becomes louder and more authoritative, and these are the ones that must be interpreted. This is when God is speaking to the church.

1 Corinthians 14:27: If any man speak in an unknown tongue, let it be by two, or at the most by three, and that by course, and let one interpret. Let's say for an example that we have a congregation of five hundred people and all of them are baptized in the Holy Spirit. When we go into worship, we can all at one time according to Paul speak in tongues to ourselves and to God. So, what that means is that we can, in a devotional way, talk to God in our prayer language or unknown tongue. In your mind you are thinking Lord, I Love you; Lord, I worship you, but it is coming out of your mouth in your prayer language. No one is getting overbearing in a loud voice.

It is not disruptive. It just flows, like a river flowing. That is private devotional, and it can be done in a service. Now you don't want five people standing up speaking in tongues while the word is being preached. That is out of order.

Then there is what we call a public message in tongues. Now we have five hundred people worshipping and we come to a point where maybe the Holy Spirit wants to convict someone. One person can stand and if you notice they will begin to speak louder in the tongue and with an authority. Now the person giving the message in tongues should pray for the gift of interpretation so that they can interpret, but if they don't interpret, there should be someone else in the congregation that can interpret. We need to know who the people with the gifts are. Interpreting a message takes faith. If you have never done it, you feel very fearful of the presence of God and of saying the wrong thing. Once you get in that flow of interpreting the tongue there are several things you will learn. Normally it will agree with the message that is taught, something which has just been said, or if God is dealing with sinners, it will be a message to the sinner. If God is dealing with backsliders, it will be a message to the backslider. If someone has preached healing in the house the Lord may come down and say this is my confirmation to you, I am the Lord God that will heal you. Sometimes it will be scriptures quoted from the word and it will make people's faith come alive.

A person who interprets or prophecies does so according to their wisdom and knowledge. Perry Stone gave some very humorous examples, and one was of a man standing with a desire to interpret and said, "yea saith the Lord, as I was with Moses and the animals in the ark, so will I be with you." When he sat down and realized his mistake, instead of standing and correcting himself, he stood and said, "thus saith the Lord, I have made an error." We all know that God does not make mistakes. This is why we need to know that we have the wisdom and knowledge to operate in the gift. It was not that the individuals were not inspired by the Holy Spirit but you prophecy according to your knowledge and sometimes you can get mixed up. This is why not many people seek after this gift. They are so afraid of making a mistake or of not getting something just right that they hold back in fear. That is why, even in large churches, you have very few people that can interpret.

I have had people come to me and say, "I got the first few words of that message, but I was afraid to speak them." I try to teach them that usually you will just get the first few words, but if you begin to speak them, the rest will flow automatically as the spirit leads. Once someone has the gift and learns to use it without fear it will flow. You can tell when someone is flowing in the gift because sometimes it will be almost poetic. Sometimes it is filled with scripture. But when this gift has been used according to the leading of the Holy Spirit it will leave a feeling of reverence in the house, as if the wind of God has just blown over the congregation.

Of all the gifts this is probably the most difficult. It is easier to pray for the sick because you can do that at any time. It is easier to give someone a word from God. You know the spirits by the gift of discerning. But when you come to this one, it is difficult because you question yourself more. You wonder, am I saying the right thing? Am I hearing the right thing? Is it me making this up? But if it is something that you desire you should seek for it. Paul said that we should desire to be able to interpret. It is a necessary gift for the house of God.

What does it mean to interpret? To interpret is alluded to four times. 1 Corinthians 12:30; 1 Corinthians 14:5, 13, and 27. To interpret in Greek means to explain thoroughly by implication to translate from one language to another. Interpretation is to explain the meaning of the message that has been given in tongues. This gift was used very heavily in the early days when I was young and growing up in the church. It used to be a common practice for the church to have tongues and interpretation on a very consistent basis. Have you ever wondered why the church seemed to change and the gifts became less operated in? I have some theories. We know that God does not change. We know that the gifts and call are without repentance. So, the change had to come from the side of the people. I believe it is partly due to an older generation dying off and the younger generation not pursuing the gifts as they should. I believe it is partly due to a lack of understanding or knowledge. As a child growing up in a Pentecostal church, I remember that the gifts flowed freely but I don't ever remember being taught to understand them. Usually if you don't understand something you tend to withdraw from it rather than run to it. Also, as people began to be drawn to the full gospel churches because they enjoyed the worship and the preaching but did not understand the moving of the spirit, it caused the spirit filled believers to hold back. Instead of allowing the Holy Spirit to work it out and lead them into it, it was just cut off. Focus began to be centered on the worship and preaching aspect and the gifts of the spirit became neglected.

I had a friend tell me one time that they had prayed that the spirit would not move because they were bringing a friend to church that wouldn't understand it and didn't want it to scare them. If you don't welcome God in, He won't come in. If you ask Him to hold back his spirit, He won't show up! If it is the real power of God moving in that atmosphere you cannot deny that it is coming from the Lord and that it is coming from the Holy Spirit. And He will draw people to him.

Now let's talk for a minute about the difference between translation and interpretation. The Old Testament was written in Hebrew with portions of Daniel and Ezra written in Aramaic. The New Testament was written in Greek. A translation is a word for word exchange, where the best English word is selected from the Hebrew word or the Greek word. For example, we go to the bible, and we read the Greek, and we see the *dunamis*. We know that can translate into the English as the word power. However, there may be a word in the bible in the Greek New Testament, such as knew; known; knowing. A word that may have a little different connotation. There can be up to ten or twelve words, each with a little different connotation. Basic meaning but a different connotation. So, the translation is to take a word from the English that is the matching equivalent to that Hebrew or Greek word. That's why we have a King James translation. A New International Version translation. Because they are translations of the bible.

So, if you look at a person who is being used as someone who interprets, the person who interprets a message in tongues, it is not necessarily giving a word for word translation. It can be, for example, Brother Charles told us last week about how that God had used him on a mission field to speak to a group of people in their native tongue. Even though he didn't know what he said, they got it word for word because it was spoken in their language. However, if it is going from one language to another, some words could be changed.

A person who is interpreting a tongue should have biblical knowledge because the biblical knowledge of the interpreter will come into play as they are used in the gift. The word style of the interpreter will come into play as they are used in this gift. Even the personality of the interpreter will come into play as God uses them in this gift. You will speak with your accent and your personality. The Holy Spirit is speaking out of you spirit and he is inspiring you, but you still have the same sound.

Paul asked the question in 1 Corinthians 12:30, do all interpret? This refers to interpreting a message in tongues in a church setting. Don't forget Paul said if you speak in tongues, you should pray for the interpretation. When you pray in tongues in your private devotional prayer language, you should pray and ask God, Lord what are you telling me? That's what Paul in emphasizing. But then he asks the question, do all interpret? He is not talking about your baptismal devotional tongue. He is talking about a public message in a church service. Not everybody interprets. As I said earlier, there may only be a handful of people in a church service that has that particular gift to interpret.

The interpretation, not a translation gives a general knowledge of what the spirit of God is saying. Notice how the prophets wrote their books. They did not all write alike. They all had a different style or a different personality. Jeremiah was to the point and very rebuking. He had a pointed style. Isaiah wrote at times very poetic. For example, in Isaiah 53, he had a poetic style. Daniel wrote as a seer with dreams and symbolisms. He had a prophetic style. When interpreting a tongue, you can have the same thing. You can have a very pointed style where you get right to the point. You can have a very flowing poetic style when you interpret. You can have a prophetic style when interpreting. Your style and how God uses you is tied in with your personality. It is the same way with preachers. Some are loud and beating the pulpit while others may just be walking around. Some can preach nonstop without catching a breath. It's a style. Same anointing. Same spirit but it is a style that comes from the personality of the person that is being used.

The interpreter's style is used in connection with their own language. A person for example from Africa or from Latin America and a person from America are in the same room, their style of speaking based on their language comes into play of the words they use in that particular language.

For example, we read in Jeremiah 2:1 where Jeremiah said, the word of the Lord came unto me saying. Then we read Isaiah 1:1, the vision of Isaiah the son of Amoz. The word Isaiah saw concerning Judah and Jerusalem; Isaiah 7:3, then said the Lord to Isaiah; Isaiah 20:3, and the Lord said. Can you see how it's the same thing, God is talking, but notice how he introduces the statement that God has given him. In Isaiah 1:1, he gives a description of who God is speaking the vision to, Isaiah the son of Amoz, the word Isaiah saw concerning Judah and Jerusalem; then in 7:3 he says, thus saith the Lord to Isaiah. Pretty blunt; Then when we get to chapter 20 and verse 3 and he has gotten tired of writing those introductions he just said, and the Lord said. He left his father's name out, he left his name out, he just said, God said. Can you see that his style changes with each prophecy, but it has the same basic meaning? God is saying something.

The key to interpretation is that it is not a word for word translation of what is said. Have you ever wondered why sometimes the length of the message in tongues and the length of the interpretation are not always the same? Sometimes a message is given very long, and the interpretation is very short. Or it could go the other way, the message given could be very short, but the interpretation be longer. In our mind we think however long the message given in tongues is, the interpretation should be the same. Would you like an answer to this? The length of a message in tongues is not always the length of the translation. Here's an example from the fifth chapter of Daniel: Daniel, with the handwriting on the wall, there are basically four words, mene mene tekel upharsin. And here is the interpretation. Mene mene – God has numbered your kingdom and finished it. Tekel – you are weighed in the balance and found wanting. Perez – your kingdom shall be divided between the Medes and the Persians. Now how do you get all of that out of four words? Because these words for example Perez means division. Tekel can mean a weight or measurement. He is taking the words and basically giving you the meaning of them. That word means weight, you've been weighed. Wait a minute that word means division, your kingdom has been divided. Tekel can mean a weight or measurement. He is taking the words and so it's not that he is taking the meaning of the word and translating the direct meaning. Mene is a numbering, so you are being numbered. Tekel is a weight of balance, so you are weighed in the balance. Perez means to divide. It means division. So, your kingdom has been divided. So, what he did, he took the words, and he understood the basic meaning of the words and from that he was able to form a thought that was actually a prophecy that happened.

Jesus speaking in Mark 5:41 says, Talitha cumi, which is Syrain Aramaic, being interpreted, Damsel, I say unto thee, arise.

Jesus on the cross, Eli, Eli, lama sabachthani? That is to say My God, my God, why hast thou forsaken me? Matthew 27:46.

Notice that the individual words are smaller or limited in number and the interpretation is a little bit lengthier. So, when you have an interpretation of tongues, remember that it does not necessarily have to equal in length, because the interpreter can be giving you a general idea or thought. If it were a translation it would have to match word for word so would be pretty equal in time. But interpretation is different from translation.

Paul's guidelines concerning messages and interpretation. Paul was concerned that the vocal gifts operated in an orderly manner, 1 Corinthians 14:33. So here are four guidelines: If a message is given out with no interpreter present the person speaking should pray for the interpretation. Wherefore let him that speaks in an unknown tongue, pray that he may interpret, 1 Corinthians 14:14. Once again I will say that this could be in devotional tongues, you should pray for the understanding or interpretation. When you stand and give a public message in tongues, you should be the first one given an opportunity to interpret. According to 1 Corinthians 14:28 if there is no interpretation given then the person should remain silent and not give another message. Paul said this however, that people praying to themselves and to God can pray without an interpreter. But in a public message, given out loud then there should be an interpretation.

Vocal gifts must be judged, 1 Corinthians 14:29. Let the prophets speak two or three and let the other judge. In line with these vocal gifts, understand that interpreting a tongue, whether interpreting a devotional tongue or in Paul's rule, how he laid out for this gift to operate, there must be an order set in the church. Remember that Paul is instructing these churches in gifts that are new to them and they have to learn to use them in a way that edifies and does not bring confusion. Where there is no order, there is confusion. God said he is not the author of confusion and will not be found in the midst of it. So, it is important for us to understand the gifts and always let God be our lead and our guide. If the Lord wants to give a word to a church or to a sinner, most of the time he will give it one time. That's why Paul said no more than two or three and let the others judge.

How do you know when to interpret a tongue? For example, in

your prayer language, when you are praying in the spirit, you will know what you are praying about. You know what your mind is on. You can be praying in the spirit and suddenly you are praying in English. That is God showing you what you are praying for in tongues. That is how you interpret the private prayer language. It is different than interpreting a message to the church. An incident happened to me several years ago, I was praying in tongues and suddenly, I started praying back in English and I was rebuking cancer in my mother. At the time I was confused because my mother had not been diagnosed with cancer, she had heart disease. But shortly after that we had her at the hospital having some test run and they told us they found a mass that appeared to be cancer. I remembered that prayer and once again rebuked it in the name of Jesus. When the test results came back there was no cancer. Praise God for moving in advance.

When interpreting a public message in tongues however the spirit will often confirm the word that has just been preached. The spirit will often use the message preached to bring conviction to a sinner's heart. At times the spirit will edify the church and the body through a believer's interpretation of tongues. So, most interpretations are to confirm the word, to bring conviction to a sinner or backsliders' heart, or to edify the church and build them up in some way.

The fourth reason that a message can be given is to bring warning. There are times that there can be an interpretation of warning that trouble is coming and that the church needs to pray. This can happen and does occasionally happen but most of the time warnings come through visions and dreams to Godly people.

When you start preaching warnings to people, most of the time they are not received. You can see trouble coming but if you try to warn people, they don't want to hear it. America is blinded. Romans 11 talks about the blindness and most of the time people want to ignore warnings that are given. Everybody wants a good word, a good prophecy and if they don't get what they want they move on down the road. Scripture says they will seek teachers having itching ears. Meaning they look for someone to tell them what they want to hear. The word tells us that while men sleep, tares are grown. There are going to be times that there are going to be warnings given. We need to take heed when they come.

We have to understand that there are times that people get in themselves and when they do, it can cause problems. That's why Paul set these guidelines. There have been times when there would be a lull I the service, maybe the speaker slows down or something and someone thinks that is a good time for the to speak. The Holy Spirit does not interrupt himself. If you remember when I first began this series, I talked about God being a God of order. He is not the author of confusion. If you speak or do anything for that matter out of order it can deflate the service. It can break the anointing. So, just standing speaking in tongues trying to be louder than whatever is going on in the church is out of order. They are not giving a message; they are just praying loudly in order to be heard and seen. Here is what Paul said about that. When the whole church comes together in one place, and they all speak with tongues and there are those that are unlearned, or unbelievers will they not say that you are mad? What a person must learn to do when speaking in tongues in a church service is to learn to flow with the congregation and that service. Some might say that this is quenching the spirit, but it is not quenching the spirit, it is keeping confusion out of the church.

It is important to know the tone and the spirit of the person interpreting. Remember that the spirit of the prophet is subject to the prophet. You can control whether or not you are angry. If a person who is interpreting rebukes in the wrong spirit it will not be received by the congregation. If they are interpreting with a conviction. that spirit of conviction will come over the entire congregation. If they are exhorting there will be a spirit of relief that covers the congregation.

There are times that tongues do not need an interpretation. On the day of Pentecost there was no interpretation publicly made because the Jews understood the language. When a message is given directly to a person and they received it and understood it, then an interpretation is not needed.

This gift is not guess work, it has to be given and used by divine inspiration from God.

THE GIFT OF PROPHECY

We are now going into the gift of prophecy which is considered to be one of the most significant of the gifts. The information that we are going to cover is very practical and very deep in many ways. In 1 Corinthians 12:9-10 it says: to another is given prophecy by the same spirit. Historical outpourings of the spirit of God have always emphasized different things. The first outpouring of the Holy Spirit on Azusa Street emphasized the vocal gifts; tongues; interpretation of tongues; and prophecy. Those gifts operated heavily through all the people that came through that revival. From 1948 to 1955 the healing revival had more emphasis on the power gifts. You saw miracles; you saw healings; you saw all the wonderful power of God being manifested in the big tent revival meetings. The outpourings we're in now and will go into the last days is going to emphasize what we call the gift of wisdom and the gift of knowledge and the gift of prophecy. Because according to the book of Joel our sons and daughter are going to prophecy. If this is so, then we need to understand the gift of prophecy. What is the gift of prophecy? How does it operate? Are there specific guidelines that we must go by according to the bible for operating in this gift?

When you think of prophecy, what do you think of? Most people think of one of three things. We think of biblical predictions that are found in the bible of things that will happen during the end times, the coming of the Messiah etc.; also, we think of biblical prophets because they prophesied, they gave forth utterances from the Lord. Also, we think of end time events or what is called end time prophetic preaching concerning the last days and the times of the end.

However, the biblical term that is used by the apostle Paul in 1 Corinthians chapter twelve for prophecy or to prophecy, actually alludes to the following: it is an inspired utterance in your native tongue that reveals a plan, a purpose, or a warning from God. This prophetic gift operates somewhat differently in the New Testament than it did in the Old Testament. Because the Old Testament prophets were used in the gift of prophecy by what we call foretelling while the New Testament purpose for the gift prophecy is what is called forthtelling. Now there is a difference between foretelling and forthtelling. This is the definition; foretelling is predicting events that will happen in the future. Meaning they are going to predict the future. This was a real emphasis among the Old Testament prophets. In the New Testament we see that the gift of prophecy is used extensively in what is called forthtelling or proclaiming the word of God by teaching, warning, exhorting and by encouraging.

New Testament gift of prophecy can have foretelling meaning to predict the future, but it does not always have that. Most of the time it will be a forthtelling or a proclamation of God with a specific purpose in mind which brings people to a spiritual result with God such as conversion, baptism of the Holy Spirit, healing, or something of that nature.

Prophesying is delivering a specific inspired message from God. In the Old Testament, Numbers 11:25-26, it talks about they prophesied. This was a group of individuals. The noun in that text comes from the Hebrew word *nabi* which means to bubble up or to boil forth. What it actually means to prophecy in the Old Testament setting was to boil forth with words. It carries the connotation of something becoming so hot that it gets to a boiling point to where it can't contain it and it has to be released out. So, if we look at it this way, God's spirit provides the fire, as in Matthew 3:11 it say's he will baptize you with the Holy Ghost and fire to where inside of that person they would boil up to where they would have to pronounce the revelation or speak the revelation God is giving them.

Jeremiah said it this way, I was going to not prophecy, I was not going to say anything else, but it was like a fire shut up in my bones. In other words, it was so burning in him that he couldn't be quiet he boiled forth. So, when you talk about a prophet in the Old Testament, when you tie the meaning of the words together, it means boiling up to a point you are not able to shut up but to speak forth. You do it not with your own words but under a divine utterance. Under the divine inspiration of the Holy Spirit.

We also find out that in the bible there are different Hebrew words used in the Old Testament for those individuals who gave forth prophetic utterances. Most of us are familiar with the men who wrote the bible, Jeremiah, Ezekiel, Isaiah because we read their books. What we don't always catch is when you read the Chronicles of the Kings, Gad was a prophet. Nathan was a prophet. But their books which they did write were never found to be placed in our Old Testament cannon. We don't know what happened but many of them wrote prophetic books. In 1 Chronicles 29:29, we have Samuel, we have Nathan, and we have Gad. Samuel is called the seer. The Hebrew word *ro'eh* and it means to see a vision or a visionary who sees a vision.

We find that Nathan is called the prophet and that word is *nabi* and it means a bubbling up or someone that speaks what is burning on the inside of him. Then we find that Gad who was a prophet is called a seer, but this particular word here is a little bit different word, it *hozeh* which means to see; to perceive; to advise. It really refers to someone who is an advisor to a king. One who would bring a word to the king or to the leader.

We have the word seer, the word prophet and the word seer used in a different form. They are three different words and each of them have a different connotation which relates to the ministry of that person and what they did. Some was a word to the nation, some was a word to an individual, some was a word on behalf of approaching the king. Someone we would call today the king's prophet.

When we look at these individuals who we call prophets we also know that there were men who were prophets of God who strayed in the bible. One of those men named in the bible was Balaam. His story is found in the book of Numbers. Balaam was called a *cosim* which was a diviner, someone who divined, not in a sense of doing it for God but by spirits. He was someone who ended up being a false prophet. That's why when you see his name in the New Testament it says they have gone the way of Balaam, it is never a good thing. What he did was use carnal wisdom and said look, I can't curse Israel because their God has blessed them, but if you take the women of Moab (he tells the king to do this) and send them down to the tents of the young Israeli guys, have them commit fornication with them, God will get mad at them and God will judge them and that is exactly what happened. So, he was a compromiser and a traitor as we would say it today. That is what made him so negative in the bible.

As an additional note there are according to most researchers, fifty-six prophets of Israel if we count Daniel. Believe it or not some of the Orthodox Jews do not count Daniel as a prophet. The book of Daniel is a prophetic book, but they do not count him as a prophet. We know from the Old Testament that Daniel according to what he wrote was a prophet. The New Testament refers to the abomination of desolation that was spoken of by Danie the prophet.

There are seven female prophetesses. Their names are Sarah, Miriam, Deborah, Hannah, Abigail, a lesser known one but her story is well known in Judaism is Hulda, and also Queen Esther. These are all considered to be female prophetesses that we find in the scripture.

The Old Testament prophet Samuel had a school of the prophets. One was located in Gilgal, one in Bethel, some in other locations where they grouped the young men together who had the prophetic gift. They were called the sons of prophets. So, when a prophet came to Israel and he had a son, his first-born son would go to the school of the prophets. It was like the Levites. They were the chosen ministers for God and if they had children, their first-born son was to take an active part in the ministry. So, when someone came to Israel that was identified as a prophet their oldest son was to step in after that dad was gone and learn the gifting of prophesying because God wanted the gift of being able to have an oracle from heaven. In other words, being able to speak through men (and women) from generation to generation to generation. So, this is why the prophetic school for the sons of the prophets was created.

If you remember when Elijah was about to be taken, he stopped by the sons of the school of the prophets at Jericho, and they said your master will go up today. They were prophets, so they knew that Elijah was about to be taken up into heaven. They knew it by revelation of the spirit of God. So, sons of the prophets were young men apparently whose fathers were prophets, or they had a history in their family with men of God. God wanted to continue the prophetic gifting in Israel by raising up individuals to learn the scripture. To learn how to flow in the worship the singing and the music which is what David did. He hung around Samuel and David could play a harp and play demons out of king Saul because there was a prophetic anointing upon him to do so.

It is also believed that Elisha also had schools of the prophets. We know in 2 Kings chapter 4:1-17 that Elisha cared for the need of a woman whose husband had been a prophet and the prophet knew who Elisha was. 2 Kings 6:1-7, Elisha agreed to build a common building on behalf of the young prophets that he was ministering to. In 2 Kings 4:38-44, Elisha was eating and preparing a meal for the men that were sons of the prophets. In the time of Samuel, we find that there was a school outside of Jerusalem, a place called Ramah, it is recorded in 1 Samuel 10:10 and again in 19:20. These were prophetic schools that were established in the Old Testament times. What I am doing is giving you a foundation on how the prophets operated in the Old Testament and then we will go to the New Testament and look at the operation of that gift for today.

The biblical prophets in the Old Testament were divided into four specific divisions. This is a general look at the four divisions.

There was the northern kingdom, which was Israel. Hosea, Amos, Joel, and Jonah were a part of that prophetic group. Then there was the southern kingdom which was Judah, or the area of Judea and those prophets were Benjamin, and others from the tribe of Judah and these prophets would have included Isaiah, Jeremiah, Obadiah, Micah, Nahum, Habakkuk and Zephaniah. Then we have what is called the prophets of captivity, meaning that these prophets dealt specifically with being in Babylonian captivity. There were two of them and they were both in captivity themselves. One was Ezekiel who was one of the greatest prophets in the entire bible if you read his prophecies, especially as it relates to the restoration of Israel from chapter thirty-seven all the way to the very last chapter that deals with the millennial temple that would be built one day The other prophet that was the prophet of captivity was Daniel, who wrote twelve chapter in our English translation of our bible that relate to the visions of Daniel that he had concerning the time of the end, the revelation of the antichrist and the revelation of the beast system that would arise in the future. There were also prophets of restoration. Now the restoration would be the restoration after the Babylonian captivity, when the Jews returned back to the land and began to build the temple and those three prophets were Haggai, Zechariah, and Malachi. These are the prophets of scripture, and this is sort of how they are prophetically divided up theologically by theologians. These are the prophets that wrote scriptures, or the inspired books of the bible.

Now moving forward into the New Testament time or the New Testament era. We have a New Testament with books that are; the gospels; Acts or the historical record of the early church; we have the epistles; the book of Revelation, the greatest prophetic book of the entire bible.

If we look at the word prophet in the New Testament it is in the Greek *profitis*, and it means one who speaks on the behalf of a God; or one who speaks as the oracles of God. We are talking about the classical Greek, an interpreter for the Gods. What this originally was, before we discover this particular word in our New Testament that was written by the apostle Paul in the list of the gifts of the spirit, was that this word was used in connection with the temples in the Grecian culture where you have the temple of Aphrodite the temple of Diana and other temples that were built throughout the empire. Most of these temples had a priesthood. In the priesthood some of them had, in one temple in particular, history tells us that there was an opening in the earth and there were fumes that came out of the opening. If you went into this enclosed chamber just for a few moments and breathed them in, you would become a little incoherent or a little loopy. The priest would go into that chamber and would come out babbling and then someone else would pretend to be the oracle interpreting what the priest was saying. The prophet in the classical sense of The Grecian culture was an individual who had an oracle from God, and he would speak that oracle out. There is all sorts of Greek history and Greek literature of individuals that were supposed to bring a revelation from their God. Alexander the Great who was the head of the Grecian Empire and is mentioned in the bible prophecy represented in the book of Daniel as that great he goat. Alexander the Great before he conquered the known world is recorded to have gone into one of these temples to inquire of the gods and it was told him that he would become this great leader and he went off of that oracle and that is what he did. Almost all of your ancient empires, the king of the empire, if they believed in the idol gods or the false gods, that really did not exist, but if they believed in them, they at some point before going into battle, right before a war, right before a crisis or somebody got sick, they would enquire at the temple oracle with someone who is classified as an individual who speaks for God. This is not in the sense of our God and how he looks at a prophet, but from an oracle of their god and how he would speak advise. Most of those people were working through familiar spirits. There were times that they gave an oracle that totally went wrong. This happened to Ahab. He sought an oracle and four hundred prophets stood before him and prophesied that he would win if he went into battle, and it was a lying spirit that was sent to his prophets, and he died in battle. Most of these oracles didn't go the way they were supposed to go. But if you were in the time of the Greeks, a world leader at some point would seek an oracle.

Remember Nebuchadnezzar, said if you don't interpret this dream, I'm going to kill all of you. So, it was common to be a so-called prophet in these temples, but you risked your life because if you said something and it didn't happen the king would come back and kill you. That's kind of a spiritual principal of the Old Testament but God said if my prophets claim to be a prophet and he prophecies and he lies to you, stone him.

What I want you to see is that in the New Testament era which in the Greek is Hellenism, the Hellenistic culture and in the Roman empire culture it was known that these temples were everywhere. And in these temples a priesthood existed, temple prostitutes were there, and somebody in there was allegedly the voice of the oracle of the god which would classify them as a prophet. Now in the New Testament however, the prophet, becomes a believer who believes in God. He was converted to the Lord and is in covenant with the Lord Jesus Christ and has been inspired by the Holy Spirit to bring forth a message from the Lord through the power of the Holy Spirit. God does not use any other method to speak except through his word and the Holy Spirit. He may give you a vision or a dream, but his method of speaking is through the Holy Spirit and if it is a true spiritual dream it comes through the Holy Spirit. So, the Holy Spirit is the source of true prophetic utterance.

Now here is a commentary from some scholars. Prophets and the prophetic gifting were used in the New Testament for the following reasons: to prophesy was to predict the truth. In other words, if you prophesy it is going to be centered on the truth of the word of God. To prophesy also meant to sing spiritual songs. You will find that in the Old Testament, men who were prophets needed to have music to prophesy. Ephesians talks about singing psalms, hymns and spiritual songs, to prophesy is to reveal and to understand great mysteries. Paul said in the spirit we understand mysteries. We know that the Holy Spirit reveals that through tongues and interpretation and prophecy; to prophesy is also to reveal God's will nationally and spiritually. In the bible some prophets were national prophets, and some were regional prophets. Some would prophesy to the king, the priest, and the individuals over the entire nation. Others would go into a town or a city and give a prophecy or prophetic word to those individuals.

In the New Testament there were both prophets and prophetesses. In the New Testament we have both men and women that are operating in this particular gift. We have Anna who was a very aged prophetess that sees Jesus in the temple Luke 2:36. We have Mary who prophesies in Luke 1:46-55 this magnificent prophecy that she gave. We have Simeon the rabbi, in Luke 2:34-35, he was also a prophet, and it was promised that he would not die till he saw the Messiah and he saw Christ as an infant when Mary brought Christ to the temple for his dedication. Elizabeth in Luke 1:41-45, this is the cousin of Mary, is considered a prophetess in the sense that she prophesied things that are recorded in the book of Luke. She was under the inspiration of the spirit to prophesy. The father of John the Baptist who is Zechariahs, in Luke 1:67-69 gives a prophecy. Do you notice how many times that it is Luke who records these prophetic utterances? We have Simeon the rabbi, we have Mary, we have Anna, we have Elizabeth, we have Zechariah all of whom are found in the Luke narrative.

Joseph in Matthew chapters one and two also received revelation concerning prophetic things. He was told by the angel to go ahead and marry Mary because the Holy Spirit has impregnated her. John the Baptist is considered a prophet, Matthew 3:11, predicted that the Holy Spirit was going to come. Jesus of course was a prophet; remember he said a prophet is without honor in his own country, Luke 24:19. The apostle Paul talks about things in 2 Corinthians 12:1, he talks about how he got caught up into the third heaven and got revelations of the Lord and things of this nature. Agabus is one of the early church prophets, he was not really a minister, he appears to be a layman, in Acts 21:10 he came and predicted that Paul would be bound and given into the hands of the Gentiles. In Acts 21 is record of Phillips's virgin daughters. He had several virgin daughters that were called prophetesses. This is a listing of some of the prophets and prophetesses from the bible. The men are called prophets and the women are called prophetesses. All of these gave forth inspired utterances. Some of them were given for a future time, some of them were given for that moment as a word from God.

We discover in the Old Testament that prophets would receive bits of insight through a period of fifteen hundred years related to the Messiah. 2 Peter 1:19 we read; but now we have a sure word of prophesy. Here is what that means; in the Old Testament the prophets all got bits and pieces but under the new covenant, when Christ came, was born, lived, ministers, crucified, buried and was resurrected from the dead, now we understand the whole picture of what all these prophets spoke of. Peter said that the Old Testament prophets searched diligently for the time the Messiah would come. Now we know the fulfillment of it. Peter said we now have a sure word of prophecy.

1 Corinthians 13:9-12 talks about how we see through a glass darkly and the reference there is to a smoky piece of glass, where you don't see through it very clearly. So, in the realm of the prophetic and the things of the prophetic we know that in the New Testament there were prophets and there were prophetesses. We also have examples in the bible of when and how that prophetic gift was used. For example when prophetic utterances occur, they can occur in the following places; 1 Corinthians 14:27 show they can occur in a worship service; Acts 13:2 prophetic utterances occurred in a prayer meeting setting; Acts 5:1-10 while a speaker is speaking a prophetic utterance can come out, in other words Peter is conducting a service and their bringing the offerings when he gets a prophetic word, it's actually a word of knowledge, but it's prophetic. He knows that they have held back money and then he prophesies that they are going

to die. He speaks it and then it begins to happen; John 1:48 it can occur within a message that's given to a person, Ephesians 5:19 it can be a prophetic type of song. So prophetic utterances can occur during a worship service, in a prayer meeting, they can occur while a preacher is preaching and suddenly, he gets a download from a prophetic word, when a message is given to a person, and it can occur in a type of song. Prophetic music is one of the highest levels of music as it comes to the anointing because it is the lord singing back to us. Have you ever been worshipping and praising God and maybe you start to sing and it's a song that hasn't been written, but you are making up words as you go? It is of the highest level of singing because its God singing over us and you are singing a song that not been written before that moment.

There is a big movement in the United States over teaching people how to prophesy or having prophetic schools on trying to teach people how to prophesy. I have to say here that you either have a gift to do this or you don't. This is not one of those things where we can just say to someone, stand up and prophesy. Here is the verse they use; Paul said that all can prophesy, but it is not necessarily saying, ok I got a word from God for you. He is talking about edification, exhortation, and comfort. Everybody can exhort, everybody can comfort, but some have taken that verse to mean, that we can teach you how to predict the future, teach you how to speak over people, and people follow heavy prophetic movements. Unfortunately, these people are normally weak in the word. The reason they are weak in the word is because they are running around trying to get a word from everybody. Here is a question, why are you seeking a word when you didn't do the last word you got? It's like a person who wants God to bless them financially and they never give when they go to church. when the Lord has told them to give. You can't get a harvest without a seed. That's just common sense. So, we are going to get into some pretty heavy things here, and by heavy, I mean it's going to be very direct and pretty strict on trying to get some guidelines in relation to this prophetic gift.

People in our culture today put so much emphasis on prophesying that people are mixing up being prophetic and receiving a prophetic word with being a prophet or prophetess. Being prophetic (1 Chronicles 12:32) is talking about the sons of Issachar and it says, And the children of Issachar (one of the tribes of Israel), which were men that had understanding of the times, to know what Israel ought to do. So, for someone to be prophetic you can understand the times. You can say this is what's about to happen because I can see this coming in the spirit. I hear the sound, like unto a man's hand, rain is coming. You just discerned the things around you.

A prophetic word, (1 Corinthians 14:25) is a supernatural word for others, simply related to the plan of God. Then a prophet is one who not only talks in tongues and gives interpretation but also has a gift to reveal the future, a gift to present warnings before things happen and a gift of guiding people through a crisis supernaturally by the wisdom of God. That would be someone who would be more of a prophet.

You are not a prophet simply because you receive a word for someone. What you basically had is a word of knowledge. Or you received a word of wisdom. Every now and then someone will say, I received this when I was praying and I felt to tell you this and that person starts saying that's it, that's it. You might think to yourself that you are a prophet. No, you simply had a word of wisdom or a word of knowledge. It does not necessarily make you a prophet or prophetic because you received a word of wisdom or a word of knowledge.

In the book of Ephesians where it talks about the five-fold operation of the five-fold ministry gifts, it mentions in chapter four verse eleven, there are pastors, there are evangelist, there are teachers, there are apostles and there are prophets. What is a prophet? It comes from two Greek words, *Pro* which means beforehand *feme* which means elevating or exerting something. So, it means going beforehand, uttering a thing in advance. Uttering a thing beforehand which will reveal something in the future or will reveal or assert a plan or something which is coming in relation to the plan and purpose of God. So basically, a prophetic person is someone who sees the information, who sees the situation before it happens. Now because this happened to me it does not make me a prophet it just simply means that I received a revelation from God.

Perry Stone told how that he had received a full color vision five years before the attack on the world trade center. It was shrouded in a cloud of black smoke. It had gray tornadoes spinning off of it. It was so clear and impressed his spirit so much that he had an artist draw a picture of what he saw. He went on tv with the picture and told that there was going to be an attack on the world trade center. When the world trade center came under attack, and he saw it on tv it was exactly like the vision that he had five years earlier. That was a vision where God showed him the future five years in advance in detail. Now as he said himself, that did not make him a prophet, but he received a prophetic vision. In Joel it says sons and daughters will prophesy. It also says old men will dream dreams and young men will see visions. So, visions and dreams are going to follow a prophetic person or a person that operates in this type of gift. In the Old Testament it was a person speaking the oracles of God but in the New Testament it was a person speaking from the divine inspiration of the Holy Spirit. To foretell and to forthtell. To reveal future things if they are a prophet and to bring forth encouragement.

The original signs of a prophet are very interesting. The New Testament doesn't give you the signs of someone walking in the prophetic, but the Old Testament does give the signs for someone who is walking in the prophetic. Numbers 12:6; And he said, hear now my words, if there be a prophet among you, I the Lord will make myself known unto him in a vision, and will speak unto him in a dream. Now this was before the bible was completed. This was in the time when the Torah would be written by Moses. It hadn't been totally written at this time. These are stories that came out of the experience in the wilderness. If we take everything that Moses said and we try to put it all together in the Torah, here are some examples of what Moses said. A true prophet was a person who lived close to the presence of God. A true prophet was a person who heard consistently from the Lord. A prophet was a person who received divine revelations and mysteries from God. A prophet was a person who had a combination of all these, not necessarily one in particular, but a combination that made a person a prophet or identified them as a prophet. A person who received accurate dreams and visions that came to pass. And a person who was not hesitant to warn people when necessary. Everybody else will go through this dream and vision stuff and that's great but when it comes to really warning people you will get extremely criticized and that is where a lot of people back up, if they do have this gift. Some people warn in the wrong spirit. You can get up and say trouble is coming and you act like, yea trouble is coming, and we deserve it, I hope God kills all these sinners. Totally wrong spirit. So, a person who hears anything from the Lord has to know the timing and the tone.

Moses made it clear in Deuteronomy chapter's thirteen through eighteen the following and this is very important because this is coming from the Lord through Moses, to write about a prophetic person or a person who is classified a prophet. Now this is the warning sign: Deuteronomy 13:1-4; 1. If there arise among you a prophet, or a dreamer of dreams, and giveth thee a sign or a wonder. 2. And the sign or the wonder come to pass whereof he spake unto thee, saying Let us go after other gods, which thou hast not known, and let us serve them; 3. Thou shalt not hearken unto the words of that prophet, or that dreamer of dreams; for the Lord your God proveth you to know whether ye love the Lord your God with all your heart and with all your soul. 4. Ye shall walk after the Lord your God, and fear him, and keep his commandments, and obey his voice, and ye shall serve him, and cleave unto him.

A prophet can give a sign and wonder and still lead people away from God through a false dream or vision. Deuteronomy 18:20 says; But the prophet, which shall presume to speak a word in my name, which I have not commanded him to speak, or that shall speak in the name of other gods, even that prophet shall die.

If a prophet assumes to speak in God's name but it didn't come from God, (this is strong), he was to be put to death in ancient Israel. Here is the reason why. God did not want people following a false prophet. So, God said we are just going to do away with you. You're not going to have a second chance to lie to the people.

In Deuteronomy 18:22; When a prophet speaketh in the name of the Lord, if the thing follows not, nor come to pass, that is the thing which the lord hath not spoken, but the prophet hath spoken it presumptuously: thou shalt not be afraid of him. A prophet speaking in God's name presumptuously that doesn't happen, you are not to fear that person. In other words, if they give this warning and say tomorrow at this time or next week at this time and it doesn't happen, God say's don't be afraid of what they are saying because they are speaking presumptuously. They are speaking out of their own spirit.

There are seven reasons for God to use the gift of prophecy or to have someone to stand in that office. There are seven reasons that we find, there may be more, but these are the main primary reasons why God will use someone in the prophetic gift. It is all about revealing the mind of God.

1. It is to warn of present danger. There are many examples of this in the bible. It would take too much time to try to name then all. You see in Daniel where the king was warned with the handwriting on the wall that his kingdom was about to end. It happened that night.

2. Warning of future danger. Look at Joel who warns us about wars that are coming. Or Ezekiel thirty-eight and thirty-nine that warns us about Gog and Magog, that has not happened but will happen in the future.

3. A warning that you need to repent of sin. Jonah is a great example in telling the city of Nineveh if you don't repent destruction is coming.

4. A warning of God's judgment that is coming. In Matthew twenty-three, Jesus is warning Jerusalem that they will be destroyed for shedding innocent blood.

5. A warning of God's blessings. How would it be a warning if God is blessing? It is actually a warning of losing God's blessing. Look at the blessings and curses of God in the law of Moses and Moses prophesied if you disobey, you're going to lose those blessings.

6. To stop a premature death. God will show you if someone is about to die prematurely so that you can go into intercessory prayer, and they can be spared from whatever is getting ready to take place. Look at Esther. God gave Esther a word of knowledge on how to stop Haman from killing the Jewish people.

7. To reveal the future kingdom, which is the kingdom of heaven, the kingdom of God. And also, future prophetic kingdoms as well. These are covered in all the messianic prophecies. Those are the words that Jesus gave. The words that Paul gave; the words of the visions found recorded in the book of Daniel of the future empires of bible prophecy. Of the book of Revelation dealing with the kingdom of the beast in chapters 11, 12, and 13. All of these things are part of the reasons why God brings a prophetic word or sends a person anointed with a prophetic gift to the body of Christ.

One of the main signs of someone hearing from God, is if they spoke, did it come to pass? The body of Christ, as a lot of people, who step out and give prophecies and when they miss it, they are not held accountable for it. People need to be held accountable when the whole body of Christ is hearing this word, and everybody is hearing God told me, God said, and it just absolutely does not happen. There may be words that come that look like this is the season for it to happen and it will be delayed for a period of time. But if a person has specifically given a word and they say this is going to happen and it's going to be this, this and this and you're going to see this happen and that don't, that don't and that don't happen, they have to be held accountable for that. Does that make them an evil person? Not necessarily they can speak out of their own spirit and not necessarily the inspiration and spirit of God.

One thing about the prophetic words that prophets give and the prophetic words that a person give is, some are conditional, and some are unconditional. Conditional means they are based on your obedience or lack thereof. Unconditional means that God himself will bring it to pass and it doesn't matter what anybody says or does, you can't change it.

What is unconditional prophecy? Certain covenant promises are totally unconditional. Meaning, God said to Abraham, I'm going to give your seed the land and this is a promise to generations forever. Much of Israel is in unbelief today according to Romans eleven, but God still brought them back to the land for one reason, He had a covenant with Abraham. An unconditional covenant that says your seed will get this land. Certain biblical prophecies are unconditional. There is no way we can pray and fast and scream and holler to the heavens and change the fact that there is a seven-year tribulation coming. There is an antichrist coming and he is not going to get saved and filled with the Holy Ghost and be on Christian TV after he gets saved. He is big, bad, ugly, and mean and the only other person that the bible speaks more about than this man is the Messiah. This man, the antichrist, is spoken of in the books of Daniel, Isaiah, Ezekiel, and Revelation. There are direct mentions or allusions to this man called the antichrist, that's not going to change. So, in other words some things are unconditional. Satan is going to be bound, he can't do anything about it, it's going to happen whether he likes it or not. He is going to go into the bottomless pit eventually, he is going to be bound for a thousand years, nothing he can do about it. Jesus is going to rule for a thousand years, it's going to happen and there is nothing anybody can do to stop it. Those are unconditional prophecies.

A conditional prophecy is like, for example, when king Hezekiah was told that he was going to die, but he turns his face to the wall and God reverses the prophecy and gives him fifteen more years. So that was not unconditional, meaning you're dying and there is nothing you can do about it. It was a prophetic word, but he alters the future by giving him fifteen more years. He eventually died, that came to pass but he altered the time frame of when he was going to die. The city of Nineveh is another example. They were told they were going to be destroyed if they didn't repent. There is an if there. If you repent, I will save you. God says (2 Chronicles 7:14), if my people who are called by my name, will pray and repent, I will heal their land. So, any time you have a conditional prophecy it will always have an if connected to it. You will be destroyed unless, if you don't repent, this will happen if you don't turn. There will be an unless or an if connected in scripture many times if that prophecy can be changed. God said to Moses, I am going to kill them all and I will raise you up, because they are sinning with the golden calf, they won't listen, they are hard hearted and stubborn. And Moses said if you kill them, kill me. And he started reminding God of the covenant he had with Abraham, Isaac, and Jacob. And the bible says, and the Lord repented of the evil he was going to do against Israel. That simply means he changed his mind. There again God made a statement, he gave a word, I'm going to kill them, and Moses turned it around by using the covenant that God had established with the forefathers.

Prophetic utterances must be inspired. This is very, very, very important that you understand, that a person don't just walk-up cold turkey (you know what that expression means), and just start speaking and prophesying. You have got to have an unction from the spirit of God to operate in these gifts. Even the prophets of the bible, it says that before they would prophesy, they would say bring me a musician, and according to the bible when the musician played the hand of the Lord would come upon them (Elisha is specifically named).

Now there are guidelines concerning the prophetic gift. The bible says in 1 Corinthians 13:9, we prophesy in part. What does that mean? It means we know in part and we prophecy in part. This is what I believe prophesying in part means. That if you have a part, you don't get everything. Because we have to walk by faith and not by sight. But the part we get is the greater part. In other words, if God is giving us a word about the danger of a trip, He may say thus saith the Lord; Agabus took the belt of Paul and said, thus saith the Holy Spirit, the man wearing this belt will be bound in Jerusalem. He didn't give him details. He didn't say, thus saith the Lord you will go to the temple; thus, saith the Lord, they will see you; thus saith the Lord that will stir them up; thus saith the Lord they will case a riot. He didn't say any of that. He had part. Part one was you're going to go to Jerusalem, maybe you shouldn't do that. Part two you're going to Jerusalem, and they are going to bind you. Part three you're going to be arrested. He got the part, but he didn't get the whole. So, most of the time a prophetic word will give you parts because Paul said we prophesy in part. It will give you the main part of what you need to know and the other has to be searched out personally through your prayer life and your understanding of what God is saying. So, we prophesy in part.

Ananias goes and tells Saul the Lord told me to come and pray that you would receive your sight and be filled with the Holy Spirit. He didn't tell him anything else to do. Didn't tell him where to take Paul, didn't say put Paul in a house, didn't say hide him from the Jewish people that might want to kill him, didn't hear any of that. When Peter was told in Acts ten by the angel to go to Cornelius' house, he went but he didn't know what he was going to preach, he didn't know that the baptism of the Holy Spirit would be manifested and the whole family would be baptized in the Holy Spirit, he didn't know really that it was the official moment that the Gentiles would be grafted in. He got a part, but he didn't get it all, because God wants you to walk by faith. Another reason God doesn't give it all to you is what if it scared you and you wouldn't want to do it? So, God doesn't give it all to you all at once. When God told the children of Israel to go to the promised land and I am going to give you this, this, and this, and it's going to be great he didn't tell them giants were going to be there. God knew if they saw those giants, they wouldn't want to leave Egypt. How do I know that? Because when they saw the giants, they ended up in the wilderness, wanting to go back to Egypt. So, God doesn't tell you everything in a prophetic word because, it's possible it could frighten you, it's possible it could scare you.

We prophesy according to the proportion of our faith. Romans 12:6, Let us prophesy according to the proportion of our faith. You can only prophesy according to the knowledge you have and the faith you have received in doing so. You don't want to step out and say something out of your own spirit, that's not from the spirit of God.

Ezekiel 13:3 says, foolish prophets follow their own spirit and have seen nothing. Perry Stone gave an example of something that happened to him, and it really hit me because I have been guilty of doing this. The Lord had spoke to him in an audible voice concerning one of his staff members. He heard the voice of God say, Tiffany will marry Nathan. So, he started looking for a Nathan but couldn't find one that matched the description of what he had seen in a vision. But one day he saw a young man going out with a mission team from his church that looked like the man he had seen in the vision, so he goes over and begins to talk to him and askes his name. It was Nathan. Then he calls the girl up and tells her, I just met your husband. So, then he tells her everything that God had told him. She begins to cry and said, nobody knows this except me and God, but I have a journal right now with his name in it. I have been journaling about him for a year. They are now married but the thing is, that Perry did not go out and immediately tell her that, because Nathan wasn't there yet. He kept it to himself, but when he saw him and it bore witness with him, then he gave the prophecy. What he was doing was prophesying in part. He got part of it, but he didn't get all of it. We should not speak something unless we know it's from the Lord. Even though Perry heard the voice he held what he heard. Because it was not the time to talk about it or even to say it. Sometimes you have to hold what you hear until the right time.

We prophesy to edify, to exhort and to comfort. The bible says in 1 Corinthians 14:3, he that prophesies, speaketh unto men for edification, exhortation, and comfort. Edification in 1 Corinthians 14:4, He that speaketh in an unknown tongue edifieth himself; but he that prphesieth edifieth the church. To edify is to build up the house. The gift of prophesy is for building up faith, for building up joy, and for building up peace in the local church. Exhortation in Greek is to call near, to invite or to invoke implying that the gift is used to bring a person closer into or invite them nearer to God's presence or God's will. The word comfort in the New Testament Greek is the same word that is used for edification, but it is more of bringing comfort to a person or comfort to a church. We console people when we comfort them. So, there is a consolation or a consoling that comes when the edification part of the gift of prophesying is being used.

One of the reasons the prophetic gift was so needed in the church was because in the early church they were persecuted horribly. Stephen was stoned, later on Peter and Paul were beheaded, so the church was under so much persecution, they needed comforting. They needed exhortation. Paul wrote to the Roman church and said the very God of peace shall bruise Satan under your heel shortly. How do you think they felt under that persecution? And here is a prophet telling them that God is getting ready to give you a victory. That is edification. That is comfort.

The prophetic gift can reveal the secrets of men's hearts. One of the reasons for this gift is to take a person in the congregation and you don't know them, and they know you don't know them, and the Holy Spirit speaks and as the old expression is, reads their mail. 1 Corinthians 14:25 says, and thus are the secrets of his heart made manifest, and so falling down on his face he will worship God and report God is in you of a truth.

Years ago, there was a man in the Northport Alabama church of God that invited a Japanese man to come to church with him. This man had never been around anything like this, he had never been to a church service. He asked the friend that had invited him, can your God tell me where my wife is? He said, "I don't understand, what do you mean?" The businessman said, "we came over here, from two different directions. Two different ways and she has disappeared. I don't know where she is, and she don't know where I ended up. But it's my wife and I need to know where she is." They go to church and at the end of the service after the preaching an elderly woman stood up and began to speak in tongues with an Asian dialect. The businessman grabbed a pen and paper and began writing. He then told his friend let's go, let's go, let's go. The friend tried to get him to stay till the end of the service, but he said no. That woman just spoke in my native language and gave my wife's name with a phone number. I need to get to a phone now. They went to a phone and called the number the woman had given and sure enough, his wife was there. They got reconnected. This is a true story. That is an example of the secrets being revealed.

We are going to look at some of the use and abuse of the gifts. Especially the vocal gifts. Unfortunately, there are people that will try to use these gifts for their own purpose. For example, there have been people who have used prophecy for spiritual manipulation. I have told the story about another preacher coming to me when I first started the church and said they wanted to help me by teaching me some things. Now this was not anybody from within our organization, but a pastor of another church and they told me, if you want to get people to do something all you have to do is say, God said. Now in my opinion, when you do that, you are using God's name in vain. If he didn't say it then you are manipulating people with a false, prophesy. You should never say God said unless you know that he has spoken to you, and you should never use God's name to manipulate people to do what you think they should do.

Introducing strange doctrines. The introduction of strange doctrines is so significant in the New Testament that Paul wrote in Galatians 1:8, But though we or an angel from heaven, preach any other gospel unto you than that which we have preached unto you, let him be accursed. It is interesting that sometimes people can prophesy, I've got a word, or the Lord has given me a word and it is not in line with the scriptures. If it is not in line with the scriptures, you have to write it off. Don't pay any attention to it.

Another abuse which I have said really bothers me is when manipulation through a spiritual gift is used to get money from people. There has never been a time when this has been done more. They say if you give a certain amount God will give you a certain anointing. Or give a certain amount and God will release blessings on you. What if you don't have any money to give? Is God going to leave you out? First of all, you cannot purchase the anointing. One man tried to do that in the book of Acts and Peter rebuked him and said you and your money perish with you. In modern language today what Peter would say is you and your money are going to go to hell. Because when he said, perish with you, that is what he was referring to. Peter didn't put up with that. So, manipulation, using a prophetic gift over someone to get money out of them is absolutely wrong. It should never happen. Now can God encourage a person to give through a word? Can God encourage that he is going to bless people for their obedience? Of course, he can. But I have seen way too much manipulation in this area.

The thing that we need to understand is that there are fakers and there are false prophets. In 1 Samuel 28:6-7, when the spirit of God departed from Saul, he sought out a witch as a spiritual method to hear from God which is forbidden in the law of Moses. A familiar spirit works through this witch, and she tells Saul that he is going to die, which happened, but it doesn't add credibility to the witch because she is talking through a familiar spirit that is familiar with the plan that is going to happen.

Jesus, in Matthew 24:11 warned of false prophets and false teachers. Peter in Acts 8:18-22 encounters a sorcerer in Samaria who wanted to purchase the gift of laying on of hands, and we know that story, that he was a false individual, and Peter rebuked him. Acts 16:16-18, Paul encountered a spirit of divination, and this was the spirit of Python as it is in the Greek dealing with a temple that existed in that city that was dedicated to the spirit of python. This woman is operating in a familiar spirit and Paul rebukes her. She is saying the right thing, these are the servants of the most high God, listen to them. However, she has a spirit, and even though she is saying the right things, it is not what she said but the voice that it was coming through. She was operating by demons. And Paul didn't want any association with someone operating in the realm of demons. So, there are fakers and there are also false prophets.

Something important for us to know is that when a faker has been exposed and people see that they were not real it makes them skeptical when the real gifts are in operation. They begin to question what they see concerning the gifts in action. Perry Stone talked about a minister that would go out and he would appear to be very successful in his ministry. He would call people out and tell them things, like their name or the name of a child or of someone in the hospital. Everybody was amazed at his ability. But later they found out that before he would go to a church, he would go on Facebook and find the pastor, how many members he had, who was a member of his church. He would write that down and make that note. He was actually using Facebook. People would post prayer request on there and he would see who was sick and who was in the hospital. He would then call out a name he had seen and say, there is someone here by this name and your daughter has cancer. When a minister abuses the pulpit and the ministry, saying something is of the Holy Spirit when it is not, they should be called out on it and banned from the ministry. Please understand that this is just my opinion but there should be accountability for what we do and speak. Even the more so when it comes to the things of God. We are to be holy vessels and abusing the gifts in this manner is borderline blaspheming the Holy Spirit. Anybody can make a mistake, I'm not talking about making a mistake or a moment of a bad decision, I am talking about willful deceit. When you plan to deceive. When you manipulate the gifts of the Holy Spirit to your own advantage. There needs to be a penalty. When ministers abuse the powers of God it makes the world look at all preachers and Christians as fakers. So, when a genuine man or woman of God gives a prophecy or message, people will start to say, I bet he talked to someone. Then God cannot operate these gifts because of doubt and unbelief. Who loses because of that? Not the guy that did it, but all of the body of Christ that should be receiving the benefit of these gifts.

I am telling you these things because I want us to understand the seriousness of being real and genuine. When we seek the face of God and humble ourselves then God can and will use us. He will also show us when something is not of him. When you are around the real thing enough and you are in the presence of God regularly, you can tell the fake from the genuine really quick.

Jesus warned us that there would be false teachers, false prophets, and even false Christ's. This is why the bible tells us to know those that labor among us. Know their lives. Know their reputation. And when someone stands up and prophecy's things that are going to happen in the future, and say God told me this will happen, you can write it down. Write it down and if it don't happen go back and ask what happened. Remember when you said that God said this would happen? Can you explain that to me? Another thing on the idea of false prophets and false teachers is, can the gifts operate through someone who is in a backslidden condition? 1 John 4:1-3; 1. Beloved, believe not every spirit, but try the spirits whether they are of God: because many false prophets are gone out into the world. 2. Hereby know ye the Spirit of God: Every spirit that confesseth that Jesus Christ is come in the flesh is of God: 3. And every spirit that confesseth not that Jesus Christ is come in the flesh is not of God: and this is that spirit of antichrist, whereof ye have heard that it should come, and even now already is it in the world. When you look at this verse that says you have to test the spirit, what does that mean? What do you test in the spirit? Let's say someone is prophesying, there are two things that you have to detect, or you have to try. One is the spirit of what they are saying and number two in the tone in which they say it. If God gives a word of coming judgment or danger and it is blasted out in anger, then it was given in the wrong spirit. God is a spirit of love. His spirit is not to have you killed but to have you saved. That same prophesy can be spoken with love, I just heard a word from God that judgment or danger are coming, and we need to pray. Sometimes a church needs to be realigned, it needs correction, but a true prophet will have a spirit of brokenness, of humility, of repentance. The thief comes to steal, to kill, and to destroy, but Jesus said, I come that you might have life and that you might have it more abundantly. Sometimes you can be in the wrong spirit because you are angry at someone. Sometimes it can be due to immaturity in the spiritual realm. Even though you have a genuine gift, immaturity can cause you to mishandle it. So, when you try a spirit, you have to look at the person giving the message. Remember when James and John wanted to call fire down from heaven on Samaria? Jesus said, you don't know what manner of spirit you are of. So, watch the spirit and the tone of which it is being presented

Test it by scripture. Does it align with the word? If it does not align with the word, you should ignore it. Don't worry about it. What are the results? God is a multiplier and not a divider. If words start coming from the pulpit and they are dividing the congregation, then it will bring confusion and God is not the author of confusion. That's why I have to be careful who I allow to come and get into the pulpit and preach. I have made mistakes in the past and allowed someone to come because they were recommended, and I lost people afterwards because of things that they said. The sad thing is that most of the time the ones I lost are the ones who requested the guest speaker to come in the first place.

The danger of operating a gift with a backslidden heart is very serious. Saul in 1 Samuel 16:14; 16:23; 18:10; The spirit of God departed from Saul and an evil spirit began to trouble him. He tried to kill David in 1 Samuel 19. He is sending men out to find out where David is so he can go kill him. He has a spirit of murder on him. So, all of these men come back, and they are changed when they come back because they are going to the school of the prophets and the anointing is so strong that Saul's guys are having their heart melted, they are being touched by God. So, Saul says, I will just go myself. Saul goes in 1 Samuel 19:23 to Ramah where the prophets are, and he is looking for David. When he gets there, he takes off his kingly robes and falls on the ground and starts prophesying. Now how can a guy that's got murder in his heart, prophesy? The answer is this. If you looked at Saul, he was relieved when David would play the musical instruments. So, the spirit that came on Saul, came on him in his palace, and came on him when he was fighting David. When he got in God's presence, he got relief. Remember it said the spirit of the Lord departed from Saul but when David played, he was made well and refreshed? So, when Saul entered the presence of God in Ramah, and those prophets are playing their instruments and prophesying, the evil spirit leaves him. An evil spirit can't stay where the presence of God is that strong. Then he returns back to his old self, of what he once was, but the problem was he changed temporarily. Meaning he never really changed what was in his heart. So, in this idea it is possible for people who have operated in the gifts to operate by habit. This is a very dangerous thing to do. You can learn to do anything. You can learn to speak, you can learn to teach, you can learn to witness. Here is an example: When you are a baby you learn to talk by repeating what you hear. Mama, mama – ball, ball, after a while you don't even have to think, it becomes natural. You begin to speak with comfort from memory. When you are saved and baptized in the Holy Spirit with the evidence of speaking in tongues, you may speak that prayer language for years. It is a language. Just like English. You speak English all the time. It is possible for a person to have originally received a gift of the spirit, like speaking in tongues, or a prayer language. But they lose the presence of God, and they can still say those words. That is a real anger. Because it means that you may falsely believe that the Lord is still with you because you can still speak in tongues. And maybe you are like Saul and the spirit of the Lord has departed from you. One of the scariest verses in the bible is Matthew 7:22-23; 22. Many will say to me in that day, Lord, Lord, have we not prophesied in thy name? And in thy name have cast out devils? And in thy name done many wonderful works? 23. And then will I profess unto them, I never knew you: depart from me, ye that work iniquity. Because I never knew you. So, can the gifts be operated by individuals who are not real, and the answer is yes. Jannes and Jambres produced a miracle, but it was a fake miracle, it's not a miracle of God. Can a person still operate in a gift even though they are backslidden? Yes, because the gifts and the calling of God are without repentance. But it does not mean that it comes from an inspiration from God, but it comes from habit. There has to be a caution with the operation of any spiritual gift. 1 Corinthians 14:32; and the spirits of the prophets are subject to the prophet. Romans 11:29; and the gifts and calling of God are without repentance, meaning that they are irrevocable.

Three dangers in the operation of the gifts of the spirit. 1. The danger of operating out of habit. 2. Speaking out of your own spirit. Deuteronomy 10:20-22 talks about speaking and it not coming to pass because the person spoke presumptuously. So, be careful that it is not just that you feel something, or you think something, that you make it to be that it is from God, when it is just your own spirit. This is probably the hardest thing that a person has to judge with a word of wisdom, and a word of knowledge or a prophesy. The best thing to do when you first get a word is to sit on it. If you are not sure that it is from God, sit on it and if it continues to build until we begin to boil over. It boils, it boils, it boils till you have to say something. 3. Speaking under a satanic thought. Now this is a wild one. Matthew chapter 16, Peter says to Jesus, you are the son of the living God. Christ says, flesh and blood has not revealed this to you, but the father did. Then in verse 21 Jesus talks about how he is going to die in the future. Verse 22, Peter starts rebuking Jesus. Verse 23, Jesus said, get behind me Satan. Now one moment, Peter is speaking by the spirit and the next moment he is speaking his own thought, which is a dart of the enemy, you are never going to die. It was not the plan of God that he never die, the plan was that he had to die, and he knew it. So, he had to rebuke the enemy. That goes to show you that at times people can get in themselves.

Some practical advice on these gifts is, let's say that I am hearing something about a situation, and I feel like it is God giving it to me, I should never jump right up and immediately begin to say what I am feeling. Now if you are in a service, you have a limited time and have to determine at that point. But, when possible, I will weigh it. If I hold it for a couple of hours or a day or two, if it's just me, I will most of the time forget it. But if it is from God, it will not leave, it will keep coming back. Let's say I am in the pulpit, and I feel that I am hearing something from God, but I am not sure, I should not say that the Lord has given me a word. What I should say is, I am hearing something, and I am going to say something, if it fits somebody here then we will know it is from the Lord and we will pray. Most of the time somebody will respond that they are the person that it is for. There have been times that I have heard a word and known exactly who it was for, but I have not reached that confidence level to speak it directly to that person. People that are used in the gifts heavily have more confidence and I am praying to there.

In the prophetic, judge what is said in line with biblical doctrine. Judge it by the spirit and tone with which it was given. Judge it also by the reputation of the person giving it. Judge it out of your own spirit. The bible says in 1 Corinthians 14, that when prophesy is given let one speak and the others judge. Why do you have to judge a prophetic word? Because people can easily step out in themselves.

If you have a word that exposes a person, you should never jump up in a church and try to do that. You expose people's problems privately. Paul said if they are causing a problem to get another brother or sister to go with you, after you have gone to them privately, then if they still won't hear you, go to the leadership if it is something that is going to affect the whole congregation. You may feel that you have gotten something, and you stand up and speak it and it turn out to be wrong, then you have embarrassed yourself and that person. You could even hurt that person's reputation. There have been pastors that have had their reputation totally wrecked because someone gave a word, and it really wasn't a word from God. 1 Thessalonians 5:19-21 says, quench not the spirit, despise not prophesying, hold fast that which is good.

I will conclude by saying that I pray that this information has in some way been a help and a blessing to you.

Printed in the United States
by Baker & Taylor Publisher Services